T0066876

AUSTRALIA TWO NATIONS

KANAGA SEGARAM

PARTRIDGE
A Penguin Random House Company

To order additional copies of this book, contact
Toll Free 800 101 2657 (Singapore)
Toll Free 1 800 81 7340 (Malaysia)
orders.singapore@partridgepublishing.com

www.partridgepublishing.com/singapore

To My Mother

ACKNOWLEDGEMENT

My **wife and son** never agreed with my radical thoughts, verbosity or eccentric actions. However, their support in my life is very precious. I appreciate and thank **Trafford publishing** and Ms Sydney Felicio for their excellent work at short notice.

PREFACE

The author lived in and travelled to several countries. He explains how Australia can reconcile with the Aboriginals in the divided country than postponing for the sake of parliament elections and playing to the gallery. He has reflected on the aftermath of September 2001 and it's relevance to Australia. Additionally, his observations from few other countries are presented. Any criticism is much appreciated by the author. When you read the book, please remember what Voltaire said: **"I do not agree with what you have to say, but I will defend to the death your right to say it."** The world has diversified opinions and standards. There may be criticisms about opinion, words or actions. The person who was called terrorist, Nelson Mandela became a modern day Gandhi. The time and place spectrum can modify the value at different points. No human is perfect. The theme of this narrative is that of Voltaire's. The civilized and matured world appreciates difference of opinions and actions. Sometimes people agree to disagree but respect others' views. In a democratic and pluralist society multiple ideas are promoted though finally all agree to the majority values. National security and patriotism should not suppress freedom of expression. A maverick or group with a radical view is termed as terrorist or hate campaigner or unpatriotic or even worse, claimed to have incited violence and disharmony. These are tactics to stifle freedom of expression by dictators and monarchs who want to be leader for life without any dissent or challenge. Soviet Union, Russia, China, Zimbabwe,

Egypt under Mubarak and Libya under Gadhafi are examples of this category. Even Hitler used Nationalism and patriotism for his ambition. In the modern democratic society, freedom of expression is highly valued. Any criticism through Facebook page and Twitter is very much appreciated.

AUSTRALIA: TWO NATIONS

"I do not agree with what you have to say, but I will defend to the death your right to say it."—Voltaire

Pope Benedict proved he was stupid within months of his elevation as Pope. He quoted from somewhere that Islam was violent. The idiotic utterance sparked world wide condemnation and protests by Muslims. Former Malaysian prime minister Dr Mahathir Mohammad aptly retorted that Christians and Pope were suffering from selective amnesia. Christian leaders forced conversion of others with burning at the stake, drowning, and suffocation. British lieutenant hung the Kandyan prisoners in Ceylon without any trial. Governor Brownrigg's aide-de-camp killed nineteen and took some prisoners. Seven of them were later executed without any trial and the bodies were hung up. During the reign of Queen Mary I in England Many Protestant Christians were tortured and killed. Catholics were put to death during the reign of Queen Elizabeth (Ravi Fernando, Sunday Times, 13 January, 2013). In the name of God, during First Crusade in 1099 when Jerusalem was captured, the Muslim population, every living thing, men, women, children, dogs and cats were slaughtered. In 1187, when Saladin captured Jerusalem, Christendom feared that Saladin would slaughter the Christians with sword and women would be raped. Fortunately, Saladin was magnanimous to display the superiority of his faith and civilization to barbarian Europe. On the other hand during third Crusade Richard Lion Heart massacred 3,000 of Saladin's men whom he had taken prisoners (Dr Kumar David of Christian origin, Hong Kong**).**

"The so-called New Nations such as the USA, Canada, **Australia** and New Zealand created by European colonialism bulldozed indigenous nations, their sovereignty and territoriality in those lands" ('Multicultural' deception of New Nations, TamilNet, 31 January, 2013**).** A Canadian aboriginal chief Spence said "Indigenous peoples have lived well below the poverty line in Canada that considered one of the wealthiest in the world" **(**Fight for rights not over, Island, 25 January, 2013**).** The atrocities committed by convicts and their descendants on Aboriginals in Australia were described by then prime minister Paul Keating in 1992 "Recognition that it was we who did the dispossessing. We took the traditional lands and smashed the traditional way of life. We brought the diseases and the alcohol. We committed the murders. We took the children from their mothers. We practised discrimination and exclusion" **(**The Australian, 10 December, 2012**).** Four years after the Bicentennial of white settlement which was not something worth celebrating for most Aboriginal Australians, Keating delivered a powerful, deeply moving and beautifully phrased speech. All the atrocities and crimes committed by settlers against Aboriginals were recognized. But that was only a lip service. Both major parties' megaphone policy changed nothing on ground for Aboriginals. Both parties have to play for the gallery that is majority Australians to win any election. They cannot afford to grant any concession to the natives. In 1998 there was an apology. Again in 2008 there was another apology. Still nothing changed for the aboriginals in their day to day life. In Bundaberg, Queensland lies an awful secret hidden under an old cane plantation outside the sugar city. In an unmarked grave the bodies of 29 South Sea Islanders are buried. Between 1863 and 1904 thousands of Pacific islanders were shipped in to toil in the state's cane fields and fruit plantations. Many descendants claim they were kidnapped by European slave traders and forced into a life of bondage. Though, officially they were called indentured labourers, actually they were slaves (AAP, 7 December, 2012). Northern Territory chief minister of Aboriginal origin, Adam Giles has proposed a plan for the adoption of Aboriginal children if they are victims of extreme neglect (ABC, Updated May 14, 2013). But some Aboriginal advocates say they are reminded of Stolen Generation. They say 'the loss of culture, land and language has a long-term impact on the social and emotional wellbeing of those children'. Deputy chief minister admitted that only one Indigenous child has been adopted in the Territory in the last decade.

In May 2012, police broke up an Aboriginal tent embassy in Brisbane. Nearly 80 protesters were dragged away from their makeshift camp by police. That was a symbolic gesture by First Nation's people or Aboriginals or sons of the soils or natives (ABC, 16 May, 2012). The Aboriginals or natives did not have any signed agreement or treaty with the settlers more than 200 years ago unlike in New Zealand where the Maori queen signed a treaty with the governor of settlers. The convicts were social outcasts not fit to be in British society. They were banished to the far away land Australia which was a colony of British. That itself could explain how the convicts would have treated the natives. The Aboriginals had lived in Australia for 60 thousand years. Unfortunately, they were not organized like the Maori of New Zealand. The natives were scattered and they did not have a leader. The mistakes Maori made in New Zealand are leaving the territory and usage of English. Similarly, the Aboriginals made the same mistakes but in greater scale. The British cunningly used the 'divide and rule' policy all over the world to weaken natives and to impose the British Raj. Many thousands of natives were killed but there was nobody to punish the settlers. As they are used to, the crusaders from Europe decimated the local population. There was no humanity but barbarism of the Christians. In 1830 there were 10 thousand natives in Victoria but by 1853, there were only 2 thousand natives. This itself highlights the scale of destruction and massacres by the settlers (Australian Citizenship, Government of Australia, 2012).

The convicts tricked the locals to fight among themselves as they did in New Zealand. Whenever, a head of a local was brought, the other local was rewarded with a musket. The Aboriginals who were familiar only to bow and arrow were thrilled using guns. This led to self destruction of natives. However, the massacres and slaughters by convicts and their descendant settlers ensured that the Aboriginal population was kept to the minimum. The alcohol introduced by settlers made the local addict and self destructive. The diseases brought by settlers wiped out further remaining natives as the natives did not have any immunity to the deadly diseases of Europeans. White colonists decimated the original inhabitants, the aborigines and then marginalized whilst their land was robbed from them. Despicable record of man's inhumanity to man was based on 'White is Right'. Ironically, Christianity condoned their barefaced discrimination and unfettered brutality (J.B. Müller, Sunday Island, 8 July, 2012). The natives were treated by crusaders like cattle. Australia recognized aboriginals as humans only in 1962 with voting rights. They were counted as humans in the national census only in 1967. The convicts and their descendant Christians were so uncivilized and immatured. Americans abolished slavery 150 years ago. When will Aussies abolish the slavery of Aboriginals? Unfortunately, Aussies are not yet civilized and matured to treat aboriginals with respect. Perhaps another 100 years are needed for the descendents of the convicts to become civilized. Every government spoke of injustices inflicted upon aboriginals but did nothing. If majority of Aussies are civilized, good natured and true Christians, then why not redraft constitution, change flag and national anthem? "I do not buy the 'good-people, bad-leader' theory; that is the theory which says 'people are good and untainted but leaders are evil'. The Venerated repositories of democracy always had a choice" (Dr Kumar David, Sunday Island, 11 August, 2012**).**

The so called reconciliation is nonsense in the current context. Australia day marks the day British invaded Australia as acknowledged by Sydney city council. Reconciliation will not take place until **January 26 is observed as a national day of mourning** instead of triumphalism. Nelson Mandela, an African languished in prison over 29 years. When he achieved the freedom for his nation in South Africa, his advisors suggested celebrating the victory. He scoffed at them and said "Don't celebrate revenge." The Aboriginal boxer Mundine said "The national anthem was composed in the 1800s when Aborigines were considered fauna. From 1901 to 1973 there was a White Australia Policy, apartheid to make Australia white. Guess what the theme song of that policy was—Advance Australia Fair. So what are they really singing? That is Advance Australia White." He refused to sing the national anthem (Yahoo!7, 29 January, 2013**).** The revised version of *Advance Australia Fair* only became the nation's official anthem in 1984. Even then the majority descendants of convicts refused to recognize the Aboriginals. The Australian constitution, national anthem and flag have no relevance to Aboriginals. **Australia has 2 nations**: Aboriginals' native land and the territory of majority settlers plus the migrants. The TV channels 7, 9, and 10 telecast forgetting the Aboriginal nation. Only ABC and SBS channels remind that Australia has 2 nations. The natives wait on the sideline and silently watch the carnivals, celebrations, elections and the main show of the majority. Mundine felt that gross intolerance prevails in Australia though racial discrimination is a crime under law and publicly condemned.

When the Aboriginals are marginalised and on the side lines how could Australia talk about multiculturalism. The talk of multiculturalism or **Pluralism** is exclusive of Aboriginals and not inclusive. Calls for **patriotism and nationalism** can easily sway multiculturalism. There have been 2 referendums whether to abandon the queen or not. But the plans for a referendum to constitutionally acknowledge indigenous Australians had been put on the backburner by the federal government until there's more community awareness and support. Julia Gillard's Government postponed the referendum to amend constitution recognizing Aboriginals. The draft Act of Recognition of Aboriginal people falls short of a constitutional convention and will not be a stepping stone to a referendum (AAP, 30 October, 2012**)**. The excuse is that the majority of Australians are not yet ready for the referendum. It is acknowledged that Australians are not yet civilized and matured. This is the truth. All the talks of unity and multiculturalism are only lip service. The Greens condemned the move though this was agreed in the MOU forming the government. However, the Greens and independent Rob Oakshore will not withdraw support to Julia Gillard's government since that will be suicidal. There is no moral value or principle or policy to be honoured. All what is important and sacrosanct is the survival of politicians. Everything else is negotiable and dispensable.

The case of Pauline Hanson illustrates the attitude and mentality of Australians. She won few seats for her so called 'One Nation' party in Queensland. The one nation is exclusive of Aboriginals. There is reluctance to acknowledge that there are 2 nations in Australia. Later Pauline was abandoned and she was almost bankrupt. She wanted to sell her house and migrate to UK. After going to UK she realized that UK was blacker than Australia and she returned. This suffices to expose her loyalty towards Australia. But what happened next? In 2010 election she lost the NSW senate seat only marginally. Isn't this proof that despite her loyalty towards Australia challenged people are ready to vote her? This is the contemporary Australia. The country needs to go a long way to become saner. More than 200 years ago French planned to invade the British colony at Sydney Cove with the expectation that Aboriginals would side with French against British settlers (ABC, 10 December, 2012). Unfortunately that did not materialize. Otherwise history would have been rewritten. There was an Indian pilot Subash Chandra Bose who wanted to chase the British from India through military means. He was very much respected by Mahatma Gandhi though Gandhi was a non violence man. Bose flew Japanese fighter plane and sided with Japanese in the 2nd world war with the hope to chase the barbaric British from India. Unfortunately Bose died during his flight. Though the population of Australian Aboriginals or the Maori of New Zealand was no match to Indian population, perhaps Aboriginals and Maori missed an opportunity to rectify the injustices inflicted by the settlers. "The Aboriginal Herbert Stahle Lovett served Australia in both world wars. He fought like anyone else, but when he returned he was denied the same rights as other soldiers. When he came back he was back to being black" (ABC, 29 May, 2012). Aboriginal Servicemen Flight Sergeant Garry Browning and Private Robert Angove were recognized only recently in South Australia (The Advertiser, 03 August, 2012).

The only protection for Aboriginals is the Judiciary which is independent, robust and impartial. If some people doubt the judiciary, they should refer to some cases. The Mabo verdict of 1992 shocked the government but the judiciary proved its fairgo. The indigenous existence was legally accepted. The Muslim doctor Haneefa was harassed on the request of UK but Australian judiciary sided with Dr Haneefa and criticised the government minister. Later the Australian government paid massive compensation to Dr. Haneefa to settle the case secretly. Thulasitharan was to be extradited to US after attorney general decided in favour of the master, Uncle Sam. The federal judge was so critical of the attorney general and saved Thulaistharan. Uncle Sam could reach any land and moon but could not influence Australian judiciary. The government's Malaysia solution for boat people was thrown out by the judiciary in favour of the refugees. The Aboriginals need to take a leaf from Green party. Though a minor party, Greens became king maker and imposed carbon tax. The Aboriginals need to form their own party like Winston Peters of New Zealand to have such leverage. Even with few seats, they can make or break a minority government in a hung parliament. The half Maori Winston became deputy prime minister.

There are only 600,000 Aborigines in Australia's 23 million population. There is only one lawmaker in the Federal Parliament among 226. Aborigines are the poorest in the world with worse health and literacy. Their life expectancy is much shorter than most Australians. Like the blacks in US, more Aborigines are in prison compared to the settlers and immigrants. The few educated Aborigines are bought over by the majority. One or two who get in to politics do not speak for Aborigines. The classic example is the Australia's first Aboriginal leader of a provincial government, Adam Giles (Associated Press, 13 Mar, 2013). If Aborigines depend on Greens, at times they may talk well but not act. The Aboriginals can dream of Chinese infiltration and carving out the northern half of Australia as Aboriginal country.

The Chinese could benefit from the resources while Aboriginals could win their country. But this will be an extreme wishful thinking as Australia is a protectorate of US with US base in Australia. The worst the Chinese could inflict would be a low scale guerrilla insurgency through Aboriginals as China does in some other countries. Then Aboriginals could be from prying pan to the fire. Already the police treat Aborigines like cattle. If insurgency starts, there will be slaughter house for Aborigines as happened 150 years ago. The best bet for Aboriginals will be judiciary and an Aboriginal party.

How is Australia's reality being described? "Australia was a convict colony sometime ago, created by a power which is not anymore! That convict mentality still rules them and they are raping the land and enjoying what they think is for eternity of what GOD has given to the world" (Gamini Samara, Sunday Island, 02 July, 2012)! "They simply rape, pillage and plunder a nation that's taken them in" was Alan Jones reference to "vermin" and "mongrels" Lebanese (AAP, 2 October, 2012). What a selective amnesia he has? Was he referring to SETTLERS 200 years ago? That is how the Aboriginals would have felt about settlers. How many cultures, civilizations, monuments and structures had been destroyed by Christians when they invaded and killed millions of natives around the world? Even in recent times US forces built their military base "Camp Alpha" on parts of the ancient Babylonian ruins following the 2003 invasion of Iraq. The legendary city of Babylon city was founded in 1867 BC. The Yankees damaged its high fortified walls and city in all antiquity. Then we can imagine how much damage would have been done by crusaders and Christians around the world few centuries ago. In Victorian-era Europe an indigenous Mexican woman was put on display because of a rare genetic condition that covered her face in thick hair. Showman Theodore Saul Rubio, mayor of her hometown took her around the United States. She was turned into an object of commerce. Her remains were sent back recently to her native land as part of the plan to send back the human remains gathered during the European colonization to Latin America, Africa and Asia (AAP, 13 February, 2013).

The '**Immigration Restriction Act' was passed in 1901 by** the new Federal Government. It excluded Pacific islanders and Chinese migrating to Australia. Actually, it was 'the **White Australia Policy'** (Earl Forbes, Island, 11September, 2012). Any person wanting to migrate to Australia must be fully European in upbringing and outlook. It ensured that 'there would be no place for Asiatics and coloureds' in the future of Australia". Australian athlete Peter Norman wore a human rights badge on the podium in Mexico Olympic Games in 1968 as two United States athletes gave the Black Power salute. Australian Olympic authorities overlooked him for the 1972 Munich Games as the punishment. Recently federal MPs paid tribute to Peter Norman for his actions. The Imprisonment rates in the Northern Territory and Western Australia are 7 Times more than other states just because more Aboriginals are imprisoned (AAP, 22 November, 2012). In one of the state's adult jails inside Port Phillip Prison in Victoria a 16-year-old Aboriginal boy was held in solitary confinement (ABC, 26 October, 2012). In Queensland 80% of indigenous prisoners are mentally ill. That means for the Aboriginals the prison is a substitute for mental asylum (AMA, 02 July, 2012). Aboriginals, feeling hopeless resort to alcohol, violence and petrol sniffing. A former pastor in Alice Springs said that their deaths are "verge on genocide". He says that the Federal Government is 20 years too late in taking action (ABC, 8 February, 2013).

In Western Australia a black man was mistaken for a mental hospital patient and given antipsychotic drugs. That means any black man identified as the patient would have been taken in and blindly treated without any check on identity. An Aboriginal man was severely beaten by several police in Northern territory. The police said there was no CCTV. But repaired CCTV showed the extent of brutality. This led the Watchdog to investigate Police cover up. Five police officers bashed to death an Aboriginal man in Alice Spring cell and later police claimed he fell down. Ultimately, police claimed that he died of 'a lung complication' (Indymedia, 7th Jan, 2012). The family demanded that police to be charged over the death in police custody of the Aboriginal man Briscoe (AAP, 02 August, 2012). The family said the coroner whitewashed the death. In spite of brutality, unsurprisingly, no police is held responsible and there will be no prosecution against police. An aboriginal man was put at the back of a van which was hot and lacked ventilation by prison authorities. He later **died in the prison van** but prison authorities were exonerated. Had this been **an animal, the perpetrators would have been punished for cruelty.** That means animals are superior to Aboriginals. "Superior arms power however does not give invaders the prerogative to believe that Aboriginals remain subjugated—mere serfs—who continue to live in a land where invaders reign as Lord of the Manor." There is RSPCA which treats animals at much higher level than Aboriginals.

"The sixth-generation Australian wanted to acknowledge all aspects of the country's history from the indigenous people through the British colonial period to modern, multicultural Australia". This statement is absolute nonsense. Melbourne University study found 85% feel multiculturalism does not exist in Australia. If the person is European, then he is good. But if it is Chinse he is not welcomed. In Hobart Supermarket giant Coles advertised for cleaners at one of its stores but stipulated 'no Asians and no Indians' (ABC, 28 August,

2012). ABC news presenter said he was racially abused in front of his young daughter on a bus in Sydney by a female passenger who called him black (AAP, 22 November, 2012). Worst of all is that the others watch and may be enjoying this sort of racial attacks. The majority will be silent observers than to intervene during racial attacks. A 13 year-old girl called the footballer Adam Goodes an ape (ABC May 25, 2013). She is still a child. The 13 year old is not responsible but it depends on parenting and schooling. Collingwood's President Eddie McGuire's excuse as 'slip of the tongue does NOT hold good as it was not just one sentence (AAP, 30 May, 2013). He suggested that Adam Goodes could take the role of King Kong. Murderers, rapists, paedophiles and other criminals always have some excuse for their action. Loss of sleep or intoxication is not a valid excuse for crimes. The board members are appointed by him and what moral they have to exonerate him? It is not 'if' but he should step down from AFL as well as from his 'hot seat'. It is the subconscious ideas which came out in public. If this gentleman is going to be re-educated as punishment, then, it is an incentive for racial vilification.

Four Melbourne taxis refused rides to a group of Aboriginal actors. The same group was racially abused again in a tram (ABC May 2, 2013). They were told 'you Aboriginal people don't exist in this country. You should go'. What an irony that the descendants of those who settled later telling the first nation people to leave Australia? A young tourist French woman who was singing a song in her language on a late night bus in Melbourne was subjected to ugly racist attack from a group of men. She was told to speak in English or die and her breast would be cut off. Mobile phone footage of the incident has drawn international attention and that is the best advertisement for Australian tourism. Professor Kevin Dunn's study showed that half of Australians harbour anti-Muslim sentiments. One third of Australians admitted some feelings of racism towards Aboriginals. In our workplaces 40 per cent of those who were born in Sri Lanka or India and 60 per cent Muslim Australians faced racism (Today Tonight, 21 November, 2012). Prime Minister Julia Gillard's partner, the so called first bloke, Tim Mathieson told to "look for a small, Asian, female doctor" for the digital examination of the rectum to exclude prostate cancer (ABC, 29 January, 2013). This moron is a typical Australian!

In April 2012 a police officer viciously punched one of the suspects from a stolen car. Police opened fire, hitting the 14-year-old driver in the chest and arm while his passenger, 18, took a bullet to the neck. Police said a female pedestrian was run over and dragged for 10 meters but the female was discharged from hospital on same day. The incident stoked fears of racial tensions in the impoverished Aboriginal suburb of Redfern. The boy with bullet in his neck and bleeding heavily was brutally dragged from car and punched several times before hand cuffed. The stupid police Sergeant noticed late the the person was dead and started CPR. He survived. There were fears of a repeat of 2004 riots following the death of Aboriginal teenager TJ Hickey. In Northern Territory mentally impaired people are kept in jail indefinitely, without being convicted. In the Alice Springs jail, 4 men are held without being convicted of a crime and with no release date because they were deemed "unfit to plead". This practice amounts to torture. Aboriginal health posters riddled with errors are recalled. These will be shredded leaving the taxpayer thousands of dollars out of pocket (AAP, 3 October, 2012). Prime minister Julia Gillard visited Papua New Guinea (PNG). The prime minister of PNG was straight forward, frank and very undiplomatic to raise the visa issue publicly (AAP, 10 May, 2013). He said that 40 countries have ETA but not PNG. The former colony is treated differently though it is a close neighbour. Is it racism? He requested to overhaul the visa system for his citizens.

AROUND THE WORLD

British prime minister David Cameron said that he would be visiting India in a 'spirit of humility' indirectly **apologising for Britain's imperial rule** there (Mail online, 3 June, 2012**)**. In 1919, British colonial forces massacred More than 300 Indians. Britain's prime minister laid a mourning wreath at the site and said the killings were a shameful event in British history (Associated Press, 20 Feb, 2013). During queen's jubilee, West Indians brought from Jamaica in 1950s to relieve labour shortage in UK sought an apology. Bank of Canada governor apologised for racial row after removing an image of an Asian-looking scientist from new $100 bills (AFP, 21 August, 2012**)**. Dutch soldiers massacred between 3,000 and 5,000 villagers in Indonesia in the 1940s. According to Dutch statute of limitations even the most serious crimes became void after 24 years. Therefore, prosecutors said it was too late to bring the soldiers to trial. In 1950s US doctors infected blacks and Guatemalans with Syphilis germs to test effectiveness of penicillin. Using the blacks as guinea pigs showed the slavery mentality and apartheid. Rodney King was beaten almost to death by 4 police officers in USA. The court acquitted police despite the availability of video evidence. Race riot that followed resulted with 50 deaths and $1 Billion loss of property. The man died on 17 June 2012. There are 566 federally recognized Native American tribes which live in poverty. Australian Prime Minister Julia Gillard fell on the ground in front of TV cameras when she visited India (AFP, 18 October, 2012). Was this an apology at the Indians' feet for the attacks on Indian students in Melbourne? But it would have been more appropriate had this happened in front of Aboriginals. She was unhurt and laughed off the incident.

AUSTRALIAN POLITICS

Prime minister Julia Gillard reinvented the wheel and released the paper advocating for 4 Asian languages to be taught in Australian schools. Kevin Rudd proposed this in 2008 and allocated $60 Million which ended in 2012. White Australia preferred UK, USA and other European countries to Asian countries. Australian immigration policy was that. Even non English speaking East European countries were preferred than Asian countries. John Howard cleverly implemented white Australian policy though apartheid officially came to an end in 1973. But that was only in paper. Australia has completely alienated the big neighbour Indonesia which is a truly independent country. From time to time, the Australian politicians as well as Dick Smith expressed concern against Chinese investment. Rich people like Dick Smith and Paul Howes can syndicate to campaign 'buy Australian products'. But ordinary Australians will buy cheaper imports. If the Chinese impose economic embargo, Australia will collapse. In May 2012 Labour trade unionist Paul Howes asserted that Labour government may be down but not out. He appealed to re-elect Labour. By the end of the month government granted permission to Gina Rinehart to import 1700 foreign workers to be employed in Gina Rinehart's $9 billion Roy Hill iron ore project. Paul Howes said he could not understand who the genius was who came up with this idea when manufacturing was closing down in Australia with heavy labour losses. This is sheer lunacy he said. The inquiry in to previous NSW government exposed how a businessman was rotating premiers at his whims and fancies. Where was Paul Howes when the circus went on for years in NSW?

Former premier Morris Lemma said on TV interview on 11 August 2012 that the rational thing was to privatize electricity in states. But in 2008,

Union leaders opposed leading to higher electricity charges and loss of NSW Labour. Union leaders though minority and few just because of their affiliation to party think they should decide policies and dictate to party. Prime minister Kevin Rudd was toppled by Union leaders in the coup of Julia Gillard. Julia Gillard and Paul Howes please note Morris Lemma's wisdom. More than a year after leading NSW Labour to its most crushing defeat in history in 2011, Ms Keneally confirmed she would be stepping down as the member for Heffron. Why did not she quit then and there like the Queensland lady Anna Bligh who resigned from Party leadership in the same night when election result was out. But after dawn the catastrophe became clearer and wisdom prevailed. She quit politics altogether unable to digest complete wipe out. The health workers pay was bungled for months after introducing new software. But Anna Bligh went to work in hospital to know their problems. Her trick did not work. People are not so stupid to be fooled by such antics. Her master chef show off and wide TV publicity betrayed her.

Labour leadership was again challenged in February 2012. Once the dust settled, there was declaration that everything was settled once and for all. Unfortunately, there was replay in March 2013. Again the same declaration and everything was buried and cremated. The Australians will not be surprised to see the same drama again just before the September 2013 election when many will desert the sinking ship of Labour party and government. The best option may be to make unionist Paul Howes as Labour party leader. He could solve the wages issue for workers while reopening the manufacturing industry which saw many closures under prime minister Julia Gillard. After the closure of many industries for 2 years, the prime minister set aside one Billion to create jobs in the election year. What a nonsensical drama? Are the voters so stupid to be fooled by cheap tricks just before election? There will be many more candies and freebies in the months of June, July and August before the election in September 2013. Where was the PM, Paul Howles and the money when the industries closed one after the other? After allowing foreign workers, PM started the campaign against foreign workers in the election year. May be Pauline Hanson is the secret advisor for Julia Gillard! Few months before election in 2013, PM Julia released the 'education reform' recommended by the great Gonski. Unfortunately, the universities were sacrificed at the altar to fund schools!! This may be the last nail on PM Julia Gillard's coffin before she goes home on 14 September 2013!!! May be the great Gonski recommended that Bill Gates never attended university, so universities could be closed down to improve schools. Perhaps Bill Gates was the advisor but no fund was forthcoming from him. Boat people and foreign workers will be the foot ball for both major parties. Mark Taylor, a councillor was humble when he disclosed in March 2013 that his ancestors were boat people in 1890. Unfortunately, many have forgotten history that most Australians' ancestors were boat people to the Aboriginals. The so called 'neo-natives' are descendants of boat people compared to the original natives, the Aboriginals. Unfortunately, migrants also side with the strong majority against the Aboriginals.

After toppling Kevin Rudd, the prime minister elected by majority Australians, Julia Gillard lost the elections in 2010. Unfortunately, selfish independents propped up her to continue in power. The Greens compelled the minority government to pass carbon tax law. Then Greens leader Bob brown retired very happily. The novice independent Rob Oakshore wanted to be the speaker of parliament without even a single day experience in parliament. He amassed votes because he was married to an Aboriginal lady. Unfortunately, the Aboriginals got nothing. The independents said no in principle but voted with government every time.Andrew Wilkie, independent from Tasmania was taken for a ride by Julia from August 2010 till end of 2011. The man deservedly got what was relevant for supporting a minority government on the basis of poker reform. When he was a spent force, as a face saving measure he supported a trial in Canberra of the Pokie restrictions. He gave too long period to be cheated when government somersaulted. The government and ministers were campaigning against unrestricted pokie. Then, unable to face the onslaught of Clubs Australia, the prime minister and government back flipped. Andrew Wilkie was left in limbo.

Both major parties accepted that Australian budget is in crisis. That necessitated major cuts to spending. Ironically the Labour proposed legislation for tax payers to fund the political parties' election campaign (The Courier Mail, 30 May, 2013). That too was back dated by few months. Isn't this hypocrisy? Fortunately, the Greens and independents came out in public against the proposal. On the face of serious back lash from voters the government dropped the idea. Once a Labour minister, Martin Ferguson announced in parliament that he would retire from politics. A well respected parliamentarian is frustrated by Julia Gillard's antics. **Are the birds deserting the sinking ship?** After September 2013 Election, Julia Gillard will be sent to back bench and Kevin Rudd will take over again. After he blew up over a hot pie federal minister Bill Shorten apologised to a Melbourne shopkeeper. He denied he swore at Ms Huang. "I certainly did exit the milk bar in search of my pie. I don't recall what I said then" said the minister (AAP, 3 August, 2012). A man who cannot recall what he said few hours ago is work place relations minister!! Unless he was intoxicated he should remember what he uttered!!! Paul Howles in ABC TV interview has admitted that Kevin Rudd was dumped based on polls but now he is not interested in polls when Julia and Labour are at the bottom in polls (ABC, 19 Feb, 2013).

QANTAS (Queensland And Northern Territories Air Service), the national airline of Australia was in turmoil due to frequent industrial actions in October 2011. The flights were on and off. Trade unions were dictating terms and government was a silent spectator. The CEO Allen Joyce did a radical surgery by grounding its entire domestic and international fleet (The Age, 30 October, 2011). He locked the workers out. His theory was 'All or None'. Federal government was forced to intervene to avert further turmoil. The trade union was shocked and criticized Allen of trying to smash trade union actions. Labour union's Paul Howes could not compel Allen Joyce. In effect Allen broke the backbone of trade unions. The whole country woke up. Fairwork Australia intervened. The employees returned to work as there was no other choice. Every industry needs a CEO like Allen, always ready to take risk. Allen is still running Qantas despite efforts to oust him. Other industries and countries should learn Allen's radical action. Royal Dutch Shell chief executive says that rising costs are a challenge for doing business in Australia (AAP, *28 May 2013*). Obviously, they are looking for some other countries. He says it is difficult to compete with other gas producers in North America, Asia and East Africa. He concurs with Gina Rinehart. Gina says mining is not a cash cow to solve all the evils of the society. She too wants the costs reduced in mining.

Ford announced that 1200 workers out of 3500 people would be made redundant this year. After 90 years in existence, that is not the only bomb shell. Ford would stop manufacturing cars in Australia by 2016 (AAP, 23 May, 2013). This is because the cost of manufacturing cars in Australia is high. There will be further job losses associated with car parts sale and retailers. This is despite the government's grant of $34 million in 2012. Is this an early warning that car industry is terminally ill in Australia? Is the car industry being given oxygen to float it temporarily before facing the inevitable? The high Australian dollar is not a major factor. Even domestic sales dropped. Did Ford make the announcement to have maximum impact in the forthcoming election and to give a slap on the face to Labour? Is this an indirect warning that wages in Australia are not viable for manufacturing? The Ford's CEO said that Australians would not support lower labour costs and therefore, the industry would not be profitable. He says it is double when compared to Europe and four times that of Ford in Asia. Holden too announced 400 job cuts after receiving tax payer's $215 million. Now, following Ford's announcement Holden would seek more government support (ABC, 24 May 2013). There have been criticisms against state and federal money given to Holden in recent times. What is the response by Julia Gillard, Paul Howes and Dick Smith? Should they be appointed as competent authority of manufacturing? PM announced $1B to boost jobs. Will this be enough to support the 1200 workers who will lose jobs? It is a joke by the PM that more jobs will be created with $1B while closing down manufacturing with losses of jobs. Can Allen Joyce of Qantas turn around manufacturing if he is appointed as competent authority?

Bob Carr, the foreign minister in 2012 exposed his dementia with knee jerk reaction to the political coup in the neighbouring Papua New Guinea (PNG). Later he back flipped that he did not mean economic sanctions against PNG. The power of a business man in NSW was exposed during the corruption inquiry. The businessman was a state minister when Bob Carr was NSW premier. However, Bob blamed his successor for giving undue prominence to the businessman. What a clever amnesia? The foreign affairs department has launched an investigation into its handling of a death of a suspected Australian spy in Israel. Israel used fake Australian passport for an assassination in Arab world. Australia could not do anything without green light from the master Uncle Sam. Zygier was suspected by Israel that he was about to expose fake passports (AAP, 15 February, 2013). The department of foreign affair and trade was not sure whether the minister knew details. Paul Keating, former prime minister said that US lost wars in Korea, Vietnam, Iraq and Afghanistan (AAP, 15 February, 2013). Therefore he suggested that Australia should not be a subordinate of US but should be an ally of China, the giant in Asia.

The so called **Australian terrorist David Hicks** could see some silver lining at the edge of the cloud. A former prisoner and former driver of Osama Laden in a similar situation had won the appeal. US appeals court ruled that the law was effective from 2006 and the driver could not be charged with material support for terrorism from 1996 to 2001 (The Australian, October 17, 2012). President Obama announced in mid December 2012 that US recognized the Syrian opposition. Within 24 hours Australian foreign minister Carr said that Australia recognized the Syrian Opposition. What further proof is needed that the master of Australia is Uncle Sam? When US submarine torpedoed Japanese ship in World War 2, nearly 1000 Australian prisoners of war drowned. On 01 July 2012, the 70th anniversary of the drowning was remembered. Why was 70th anniversary remembered while forgetting 50th or 60th? The bombing of Darwin by Japanese was remembered on the 70th anniversary but not 50th or 60th. Why? On 4 April 2012, about 200 US marines arrived in Darwin to be followed by 2500 personnel. But labour government denied Darwin would be a US base. The Microsoft's X Box secrets were published by an Australian teen ager. His home was raided and possessions seized by the US Federal Bureau of Investigation and Australian Police (The West Australian, 23 February, 2013). Uncle Sam could reach any territory on earth whether sovereign or not! In June 2012, former PM

Malcolm Fraser said Australia should act independently than a tail of US. In August 2012 he said Australia should NOT have gone for war in Iraq. When Australia reduced defence budget US expressed concern. But Australian defence minister and prime minister bluffed. Despite that Hilary Clinton was accorded head of state reception as Uncle Sam is the master of Australia.

Former prime minister Paul Keating said Australia should focus on Indonesia than being subservient to the United States. He said former prime ministers John Howard, Kevin Rudd and Julia Gillard had damaged Australian independence and hurt relations with Asia (ABC, 15 November, 2012). Howard described himself as a deputy sheriff while being closer to Asia. Australia had become a US colony, backyard and 52nd state. Labor government was nervous about the announcement that US Marines would be based in Darwin, ahead of President Barack Obama's 2011 visit (AAP, 5November, 2012). Obviously Master can do anything and the colony can only grumble. Japanese are involved in whaling despite a ban. The 'Green Peace' ship was trying to disrupt the whaling. Japan sent its navy to escort whaling. Australia said it would seek legal remedy. Obviously, Australia has to get green light from Uncle Sam before sending their navy.

PM Julia Gillard flew to UN HQ to canvas for a seat in Security Council competing with Luxemburg and Sweden. Australia's international importance can be judged that last time Australia had a seat in Security Council was in 1984. After 28 years and spending $24 Million to secure a seat which runs only for 2 years shows how important is Australia on world map. Julia claimed that Australia contributed in Iraq and Afghanistan. So she requested for a payback for the sacrifice of Australian soldiers! Opposition leader Tony Abbott mocked that

$24M for a bronze medal was not worth. During her speech PM warned Iran and Syria. This is like the Office boy (Australia) of an executive (US) warning independent Managers (Iran & Syria). The PM was canvassing African countries for a seat. Australia which treats its own blacks worse than animals was canvassing world blacks to get a seat.

Foreign Minister Bob Carr said it was an endorsement of Australia's good global citizenship and a "lovely moment" when Australia won 140 votes to upset Finland—108 and Luxembourg—128, in the first round of voting by the 193 UN delegates (AAP, 19 October, 2012). What was NOT publicized was that Rwanda, an African country harbouring war criminals got 148 votes. Imagine the plight of Australia in world affairs. Julia Gillard wanted to vote against Palestine observer status at UN. But after ministers objected, the government decided to abstain. After getting a seat in Security Council, the first thing Australia achieved was running away from voting on this important issue to please the master Uncle Sam. UN voted overwhelmingly to accommodate Palestine as a non member state. France voted in favour but Australia, the dependant country abstained on this crucial vote after ascending to Security Council seat (Sydney Morning Herald, 1 December, 2012).

Democracy forum was held in Bali in mid November 2012 and was co chaired by Julia Gillard. That was an irony that the lady who violated democratic principles in July 2010 by back stabbing Kevin Rudd who was overwhelmingly elected as PM by popular vote was talking about democracy. During APEC summit in Russia Prime Minister Julia Gillard revealed that Australian embassy complained to Moscow regarding the imprisonment of the rock band Pussy Riot (ABC, 8 September, 2012). The 3 women were jailed after performing a protest song against Russian president Vladimir and charged for "hooliganism". What an irony? Julian Assange an Australian is left to mend his own but PM is worried about 3 Russians. Obviously Australia, a colony of US is unable to raise Assange's case but can raise the issue of 3 Russians. What a duplicity and hypocrisy? Aboriginals are imprisoned for trivial matters in Australia but Julia is trying to protect Russian singers. What an irony? Melinda Taylor who represented the defendant Gaddafi's son at ICC was held in Libya for weeks despite the rhetoric and a visit by FM Bob Carr. Australia agreed to restore full diplomatic relations with military run Fiji which was suspended from commonwealth. Military coup leader Voreqe Bainimarama is still dictator but Australian diplomacy has rewarded him after 3 years.

There was fanfare when PM announced the National Broadband Network (NBN) costing 40Bn dollars. After 3 years still there is no light at the end of the tunnel. Even the NBN website is unable to predict when some suburbs will get broadband. It could face 10 year delay and budget blowout (ABC, 22 Mar, 2013). Suddenly, the Asbestos was dug out from sites where Telstra laid fibre optic cables. Now this has become a monster which necessitated halting of NBN work at more than 100 sites. Bill shorten announced that all those affected by Asbestos will be compensated. This has become another debacle like the ceiling insulation mania. There was controversy that PM, when she was a lawyer acted improperly. She handled her union boyfriend's matter which a prudent lawyer would have handed to another lawyer. Further she did not open a file and failed to inform the partners of the law firm Slater & Gordon. A more prudent lawyer would not have had to leave Slater & Gordon in the circumstances of Gillard's departure (The Australian, 05 December, 2012). On 23 August 2012 press conference Julia Gillard swallowed her own words few days earlier that allegation of professional misconduct in 1995 was not worth replying. She always denied that she did anything wrong. But she never explained why did she leave the law firm. Peter Slipper an opposition MP was being investigated for improper conduct by the Liberal party. Then, he joined government ranks. He was elected speaker of the house by the government. There was a sexual harassment case against the speaker by one of his staff. Slipper broke down in courts saying that his marriage, career and finances were being damaged because of the case. The staff sued the government as well. While Peter Slipper's case was going on in courts, attorney general (Rocky) Nicole Roxon was giving press meeting explaining that the speaker's staff was instigated by opposition party. Though it was sub-judice she dared to talk to press. Unfortunately, in a U turn the government settled the case by paying $50 thousand to the staff and promising in court to give more training to MPs on sexual harassment. Nicola Roxon's office issued an apology after confirmation that Attorney General's office granted Mr Slipper access to the car park (ABC, 5 October, 2012).

Once Slipper's sexy texting was revealed, the speaker resigned. When Peter Slipper's case was thrown out of courts as politically motivated, Rocky Roxon again uttered gospel truth that her and Govt's stand was vindicated. Then why did Rocky Roxon settle the case, pay $50K and also most importantly agree to train MPs on sexual harassment? When police filed charges against slipper for cabby charge fraud, Rocky Roxon forgot to open her mouth. These charges were initially made by his staff. In defending Slipper, PM ditched all ethics and principles in an effort to hang on to power (The Australian, 12 October, 2012). Sydney Morning Herald Editor said the PM had 2 choices, either to defend women's rights and dignity OR defend the numbers in parliament. But she chose to defend numbers and let down women (AAP, 10 October, 2012). It was announced that federal independent MP Peter Slipper had joined Clive Palmer's United Australia Party (ABC, 11 May, 2013). But within 24 hours Slipper was dumped by the party. If there is one man who can bring down the new party, it is Slipper. Craig Thomson, a government MP was facing multiple charges of fraud while he was a health union official. Later he submitted evidence of phone hacking as a defence for calls made from his phone to prostitutes. Does the evidence say his phone was hacked? Labour party doled $350 thousand to him so that he would not be insolvent to lose his seat though he was suspended from party. Now, he is planning to contest forthcoming election as an independent candidate. But more than 100 charges against him are pending. Government minister Macklin said during a press meet that she'd be able to live on the dole government was paying unemployed. But the transcript was released minus that part. Later she apologised, admitting her remarks were insensitive (AAP, 11January, 2013). It showed how far she was out of touch with reality.

Australian federal Court denied US request to extradite Santhirarajah, ruling that the US charges against him were "political". The judge criticized Attorney general Rocky Roxon for denying procedural fairness. The attorney general erred in the way she accepted extradition would not result in torture and failed to properly consider the best interests of Santhirarajah's son (TamilNet, 01 September, 2012). It is not surprising Australia is a tail of US. We saw that abundantly clear during PM Julia Gillard's knee jerk reaction about Julian Assange's case at the very first instance. She said Assange was guilty of illegal activity in the Wikileaks. Despite being a lawyer, she echoed the master's voice. Few days later FM Kevin Rudd set the record straight that based on Julian's presumption of innocence Australia would give consular support. Later this was amply demonstrated when Julia Gillard said Assange got consular support like any other Ausssie. Later she back flipped that there was no face to face consular contact since it was not requested. How the Australian buffoons dance to US circus master? Julian Assange sought asylum in Ecuador embassy in London on 19 June, 2012.What an irony? Australian citizen cannot trust his government which wags its tails at the whims and fancies of US. "The Ecuador government consulted US, Sweden and UK but ignored Australia" said a green MP criticising Australian government for failure to protect Assange. In August 2012, when UK warned of storming Ecuador embassy, Nicola Roxon Attorney general of Australia said it was a matter for Assange, Sweden, UK and Ecuador and nothing to do with Australia. But in case of convicted drug smuggler Corby, Julia requested Indonesian president for clemency. What a double standard? How can Australia raise voice against US Master? An Aboriginal Nation's passport was offered in an inner-city Sydney ceremony to WikiLeaks founder Julian Assange after he was "abandoned" by Australian government. Ray Jackson said "the **Australian government is quite happy to sit back and take orders from the US"** (AAP, 15 September, 2012). Only Green party supported Assange. It said the government had not done enough and he should be directly supported. Australia believed US wants to prosecute Assange despite Foreign Minister Bob Carr's insistence that the US was not pushing for Assange to be pursued over the leaks. He refused to promise that US would not target Julian. In September 2012 UK foreign secretary William Hague threatened to raid the Ecuadorean Embassy in London and drag out the WikiLeaks founder for extradition to Sweden (Sunday Island, 09 Sept, 2012). Later saner counsel prevailed that there could be retaliatory attacks in the Arab world. Remember the US embassy staff were taken hostage in Iran.

OLYMPICS 2012

The July 2012 London Olympics depicted British history, culture, heritage and past achievements. As Malaysian ex Prime minister Dr Mahathir said, selective amnesia conveniently omitted the atrocities, crimes against humanities and **killings in the name of Jesus committed by British** in Asia, Africa, Americas, Australia and New Zealand. Why did they forget to display slavery committed in the name of Jesus? The residents of a London apartment tower went to court in a bid to stop their rooftop being used as a missile base during the Olympic Games (Associated Press, 9 July, 2012). Land, air and sea defence arrangement reminded Baghdad or Kabul than Olympics in London. Why? Atrocities committed against Muslims warranted such battle field arrangements. George Michel who was charged for sexual assault, drug possession and driving under influence of drug sang at Olympics 2012 closing ceremony. A convicted criminal who declared insolvency to avoid payment to victim was selected to represent Australia in 2012 Olympics. It did not matter whether Shamedar won or lost at Olympics. It was the principle and morality that was compromised. Unlike soccer, Rugby and Cricket, amateurism and once in 4 years action in athletics led to under achievement at Olympics. North and South Koreas were rebranded by Australian daily newspaper as "Naughty Korea" and "Nice Korea" in their standing medal count. There was a response that as long as it is fine to refer to Australians as the dumb, drunk and racists, naughty Korea and nice Korea is fine. Aussies becoming boozers and weather junkies is recognized all over the world. Australian rower offered a personal apology and paid $2,000 to the owners of two shops he damaged after booze in London.

ROYALS

How many millions would have thought Camilla was a disgrace not only for Royals but also for Briton? What was her place in Olympics? She is a symbol of disgust and disgrace. When Charles becomes King, Camilla will be Princess CONSORT and NOT Queen according to myths clearance website Clarence. Charles is a stigma for any society but he is still decorating the royals. What a shame?? The 91 Year old Prince Philip told a young lady of his grand daughter's age that he would be arrested if he unzipped her dress. This buffoon was gagged not to utter anything in public. Once after a shooting death he said even a cricket bat could be a weapon and downplayed the effects of gun. This clown should have been banished from Briton but he clings on to royals. Prince Charles and Camilla encountered a few unexpected surprises during Sydney visit. A Soldier collapsed during Camilla's visit. The soldier may have collapsed thinking why was he giving honour to the symbol of shame and disgrace. It is very distasteful to have this pair touring Australia as royals. Months after Briton saw worst riots due to increase in University fees and cost of living, Queen's diamond celebration wasted billions of pounds. Queen's 60 years celebration had nothing to do with average Briton. A lady said on TV "It is the celebration of the riches".

The queen was not sensitive when Diana died. Flags were put at half mast after public anger. When Charles was having affair with Camilla Parker, the queen remained silent. When Diana confessed of an affair in BBC interview, the Queen ordered divorce the following day. What a hypocritical Mother in Law? In June 2012, Prince William said "she is grandma first, queen second'. What a realistic assessment when comparing her order for Diana's divorce? What was the role of the

Queen in the divorce of her most children? Indra Gandhi abolished the remnants of monarchs in India in 1970s. In this modern era, monarchs who are luxury dinosaurs need to be kept at museums for historians, archaeologists and antique collectors to deal with. The refreshed Girl Guides' promise will see its 28,000-strong group promise to do away with Queen. Also, the Queen was abandoned since 1993 during citizenship oath. The British may not abandon the queen due to fear of the monarchy being shifted from London to Vatican. Even after their empire collapsed, the British cling on to queen as they are unable to accept the reality. The rudimentary queen will remain for a decade or more until the British become realists and matured. Charles should be bypassed and Prince William should occupy the throne.

INTERESTING CASES

Shamewar was once caught for doping. He claimed that he did not know what his mother gave him to drink. What a clever excuse? Once he was slapped one match ban and $4500 fine for pulling T-shirt and throwing ball which hit the Caribbean Samuel. As usual Shamewar said it was accidental hit and not deliberate throw. Nobody believed him especially Cricket Australia. Shamewat was barking at a Caribbean cricketer. The Caribbean gentleman turned, stared at the Aussie and walked away. Had the Caribbean raised his bat, Imagine how ugly would have been the scene. The Aussie was fined part of his match fee. There was allegation that Australian champion jockey Damien Oliver placed a bet via a third party on a rival horse (Reuters, 20 Nov, 2012). Racing Australia postponed the inquiry until the Melbourne cup in November 2012 was over so that jockey is not excluded from the race. Ironically, after inquiry, racing Australia imposed a ban for 10 months so that the same jockey could participate in November 2013 racing. Isn't this a mockery? This is a big joke and an incentive for others to do the same! Lady ShameMac was caught for drunk driving. She told police that she did not know that what she drank at a party was cocktail. It is more serious than drunk driving. A chef escaped with burns to his body while his wife and 3 children were burnt to death. Is this fiction or fact? Compare this to a 13 year old boy who went inside and saved his brother from burning home in Gold Coast in Nov 2012. A Pakistani-born couple were jailed for life by a British court for murdering their "westernised" teenage daughter in an apparent honour killing. Compare this with killing of witchcraft magicians especially females by white barbarians few hundred years ago.

A gunman killed **26 people** including **20 children** in the Connecticut school. US President Barack Obama wiped away tears and struggled to compose him (AFP, 15 December, 2012**)**. The tears usually drain towards the nose end but Obama was wiping the outer end of eyes! Was this drama or real tears? How could US prevent mass shootings which occur periodically? Give a gun to all adults! If a person shoots more than one, then other gun holders can immediately shoot the gunman! Thus mass shooting would not happen but only single or dual deaths due to shooting. The constitutional right of gun licence cannot be revoked to prevent such mass shootings. Instead every adult should be promoted to hold a gun. If a gunman shoots at another, other gun holders must shoot the gunman and kill. Then there will be no more than 2 deaths. That is DETERENCE. There was mass mania in US that **biofuel** was greener than petroleum. Only one human said that using human food to run vehicles was a **crime against humanity**. The power of Catholic church in Philippines was very obvious when Joseph Estrada, an elected president was deposed. The uncatholic Estrada was removed illegally. The vice president Gloria Arroyo earlier resigned from vice presidency. When Estrada was forced to quit, the vice president post was vacant. There was no way the ex-vice president Arroyo could be sworn in as a president. The church and judiciary colluded to install an unelected person as president. The chief justice or the speaker should have been the interim president. This contrasts to the situation in Indonesia when Gus Dur Rahman was impeached. Megawati was still vice president. Therefore she could be elevated as president.

Two Australian radio hosts prank called the hospital where Princess Kate Middleton was being treated. They succeeded in pretending to be Queen and Charles. Later the Indian nurse who passed the call was found dead. Then in the mass hysteria, there were calls to parade the two hosts before international criminal court. Just because a depressed nurse committed suicide did not make the call a crime. It was a joke and fun call. It was the hospital that failed to counsel the nurse. Her colleagues noticed she was withdrawn and isolated but nothing was done. Few weeks later saner counsel prevailed and no action was taken against the two hosts. Pakistan prime minister Nawab Sharif dismissed Army general Musharaff and failed. After few years, the cycle returned. The then President, Musharraf tried to sack the Chief Justice and failed. There was a vast mobilization of the general public by the opposition parties that eventually led to President Musharraf's exile. Pakistani court summoned Musharraf alleging treason by suspending the constitution and sacking senior judges, including the chief justice (Associated Press, 8 Apr, 2013). Bangladesh sent one time army general and coup leader Ershad to prison despite being a young democracy. Pakistan's democracy will be tested if the same happens to Musharaf.

ISLAMOPHOBIA

In September 2012 Muslims clashed in Sydney with police who aimed capsicum spray at protesters. The riots were sparked by an anti-Islamic film which was produced in USA by a Coptic church member and depicted prophet Mohammad as womanizer. There were signs reading "Behead all those who insult the Prophet". NSW premier ordered Family and Community Services Minister to investigate the background of a young child who was pictured holding one of the posters. "We cannot incite our children to violence for any reason, and we cannot use our children to promote messages that incite people to violence" the minister said. Then, why are the school children paraded on ANZAC day? Violence is violence which cannot be justified under any circumstance. The Labour government requested Google Australia to block access to the film. Unfortunately Google said the video did not breach its content guidelines and refused to block (The West Australian, 18 September, 2012). One said that what Muslims practiced was different from what Mohammed preached. Mohamed's teachings had been transgressed, redone and wrongly interpreted without giving proof of the claim. Treating women only as sex symbols was due to the male folk, down the ages changing the laws and preaching what they wanted for their own advantage (Sunday Leader, 03 March, 2013). Polygamy may have nothing to do with Islam. It may be a geographical and historical phenomenon. When most males perished in war in the Middle East, polygamy restored the balance of population.

Serving and former defence personnel talked on social media of killing Muslims after Sydney protests. One reference of an Australian who served in Afghanistan was using machine guns and a sniper rifle on Muslims who rioted (ABC, 26 September, 2012). The police crushed the Muslims' riot with iron fist but what was the action taken against defence personnel? Atheist men were wearing SS Nazi insignias and draped in Australian flags in Melbourne following Muslim protests (AAP, 23 September, 2012). In response police were concerned that racial violence like that of the 2005 Cronulla riots could erupt. White "home-grown" Australians were called to respond violently to protests by Muslims. Provocative messages and planned retaliation were shown on Facebook pages (ABC, 21 September, 2012). There is a Dutch politician Geert Wilders embarking on crusade against Muslims. There were 8 crusades in history to deliver the holy places from Mohammedan tyranny. The Dutch delivered speeches in Sydney and Melbourne saying Sydney was Islamized. There was an interview with the Dutch on ABC radio. Later there was a hacking attack on ABC, leaking the personal details of thousands of Australians (AFP, 27 February, 2013). Turkish prime minister said "There is no moderate or immoderate Islam. Islam is Islam and that's it."

CHRISTIANITY

The legislation allowing women priest to be appointed to the General Synod of the Church of England was rejected (Anglican Ink, 20 November, 2012). Those who talk of freedom of Muslim women do not practice what they preach. A Brother convicted of child sex abuse in 1997 was referred to as a "treasure" in a Patrician church publication (ABC, 27 November, 2012). What a great tribute to a sex criminal? The head of Patrician Brothers admitted protecting another brother who committed child abuse (7 News, Sydney, 27 November,

2012**)**. Sydney Catholic Cardinal George Pell's assertion that Catholic church dealt with child sex abuses satisfactorily deserves him to be paraded before International Criminal Court. However, that should be left to the victims and Catholics to determine. Otherwise, the Catholics could interpret any action by wider society as an ambush by Anglican church. Does that mean the wider society should turn a blind eye? Retired bishop Geoffrey Robinson says Cardinal George Pell is an 'embarrassment' and he should not speak for Catholic church in Australia (ABC, 14 November, 2012**)**. Catholic Cardinal George Pell was the subject of renewed calls for his resignation and a nationwide royal commission to investigate decades of sexual abuse of children. Kevin Lee, a former New South Wales priest was a witness to a "system of cover-ups" within the Catholic Church to hide child sexual abuse (ABC, November 10, 2012**.** Bowing to pressure New South Wales Premier announced an investigation into child sex abuse by the Catholic church (AAP, 9 November, 2012). After a request from the Victorian parliamentary inquiry into child abuse the Catholic Church will release internal files on child sexual abuse within the clergy (ABC, 9 November, 2012). "**God is at fault**" claimed a former Catholic priest David Edwin Rapson when a fellow priest urged him to resist molesting boys at a Victorian school (AAP, November 14, 2012)! What a gospel truth!! Then, the federal government announced a national inquiry in to child sexual abuse by a Royal commission. The piece meal inquiries are waste of time, energy and money. International Commission of Jurists or some form of worldwide inquiry is required to cover other countries which are plagued by child sex abuse by the Catholic church. A British cardinal resigned after allegation that he had inappropriate behaviour towards other priests (AFP, 4 March, 2013). Butler Paolo Gabriele leaked documents claiming sexual abuse, cover up, corruption, mismanagement and cronyism within Vatican. Pope Benedict may be embarrassed by sexual abuse cases cropping in countries one after other. Vatileaks was insult to the injury. Pope Benedict, who claimed he would clean up Vatican when he was elected, resigned, unable to cope with sex scandals and financial irregularities (AFP, 12 February, 2013. Will the Vatican mafia open up for transparency? Then, not only the Pope's head but also several other heads will roll! The previous pope John Paul remained until death but Pope Benedict left early with frustration. Should they abolish celibacy for their own survival as suggested by Professor Paul Mullen (AAP, 15 March, 2013)? Is Vatican the worst mafia in the world? Catholics missed an opportunity to reform by electing an orthodox and conservative elderly as Pope in 2013.

"Biblical story of Adam and Eve is a myth. It was not a matter of science but rather a mythological account" declared Cardinal George Pell (*ABC's Q&A* program, 09 April, 2012). Similarly, resurrection of Jesus is a myth. Unfortunately Cardinal will not accept that since the whole of Christianity is founded weakly on this so called miracle. Buddhism, Hinduism and Islam do not have such a weak and illogical foundation. Morris, University of Minnesota said about Easter "the day Christians everywhere set aside to celebrate the day they were hoaxed by a gang of Middle Eastern charlatans into believing a local mystic rose from the dead" (**Sunday leader, 08 April, 2012**). St. Paul said to the people of Corinth in Greece "For if the dead are not raised, neither is Christ" (Fr. Augustine Fernando, Sunday Island, 31 March, 2013). How many thousands of years the Christians will wait and see whether Gabriel resurrects all the dead? Many experts confirmed by carbon dating that Shroud of Turin was from 13th or 14th century (AAP, 31 March, 2013). Obviously the cloth had been added later with the story of resurrection. Even many declarations in Bible were added later according to the geography and history of the region.

Jehovah's witnesses do not agree with the December Christmas and do not celebrate. They believe that Jesus was born in October. According to Jehovah's, Jesus instructed to celebrate only his death and not birth (The Watch Tower, 1 December, 2012). Jesus was the only one created directly by God. That means the Bible story of Adam and Eve are fictions. If Jesus was the son of God, there is no mention of God's wife. According to Bible there were 8 resurrections. Then Jesus was no special. In Argentina, in April 2012, a premature baby had been declared dead. But 12 hours later the baby was found alive in the morgue. The same month, in Melbourne, a man who was a car crash victim was declared dead by paramedic. Later he survived and was discharged from hospital after making a remarkable recovery. An elephant foetus which was declared dead by an Aussie veterinary in Sydney Zoo was born alive later. In Chile, all 33 miners who were underground for more than 2 months and six rescuers were pulled out safely in October 2010 (Sydney Morning Herald, 14 October, 2010). While the rescue of miners was going on, Pope was busy telling a fairy tale about the Australian Mary MacKillop. Pope declared that MacKillop was a saint and forgot the 33 miners. A multi story garment factory in Bangladesh collapsed. There were thousands of workers under the rubble. The death toll soared to 1200. (AFP May 10, 2013). After 17 days rescuers pulled a woman alive from the ruins. In Saudi Arabia, a car smashed and wiped out the entire family. Doctors thought a toddler had also died in the crash (The West Australian May 20, 2013). He was put in a body bag and taken to the morgue. Then, the workers noticed the bag move. The childs is still alive! Are these miracles????

Baptist church actively supported slavery and white supremacy in the name of Jesus. However, in June 2012, a black priest was appointed for the first time in US history. Pastor Stan Weatherford of the First

Baptist Church in Crystal Springs, Mississippi refused to wed a black couple (AFP July 30, 2012**).** Anglican Church denies that the new wedding vow in which **woman pledging to 'submit'** to her husband is sexist (ABC, 25 August, 2012). Is this Sharia law? Full cemeteries may force the New South Wales Government to re-use graves (ABC, 21 December, 2012**).** Isn't it against Christianity? Will Gabriel resurrect them? Unfortunately, Christians and Muslims copied the Egyptians who buried dead in special pyramids. After thousands of years, the dead remain as mummy. Fortunately, Hindus knew that dead body was meat and cremated for the last thousands of years. Hindus misled Christians and Muslims that there were 7 worlds above and another 7 worlds below. Jews believed for thousands of years that Jerusalem was the centre of the Earth. In a sphere every point is a centre. So the Jews' belief was not wrong. That was not surprising compared to Americans who believed until the 1970s that a tiny Island was China.

The Europeans believed that heart was the source of thoughts and emotions. Even now, the heart, the mechanical pump symbol is used to indicate love. The thin membrane over which heart sits and separates the chest and tummy was named diaphragm (dia-seat, phragm—mind). Hindus knew for thousands of years that brain was the seat of thoughts, extra ordinary powers and emotions. They focussed on forehead to acquire extra powers. Unfortunately, the Hindus paid extra attention to anus and called it 'moolam' or origin. In November 2012, at St Paul's Cathedral Anglican church at Burwood, Sydney a Christian wedding was officiated by a Christian reverend with exchange of rings. Then Hindu tradition was followed with tying of "Thali", the nuptial chain. These are converted Christian families still unable to give up Hindu traditions. Dr Hakim, a lecturer from Iraq was teaching in Brunei. He did his doctorate in South India.

According to him, the Muslims in India are virtually Hindus as most of their practices and customs still resemble the Hindus.

If a literal interpretation of the Bible is applied, the millions of years of Earth's existence cannot be explained. So children in US schools are being taught that Darwin's theory of evolution is wrong and Biblical monster Nessie is real. A lady on Australian TV said that Bible could not be taught in schools since it declared that the earth was created in 7 days. Mormonism has a history of supporting polygamy, racism, sexism and slavery. Philippine Catholics protested against the proposed birth control law (AFP, 05 Aug, 2012). Angry Catholics have accused an Indian sceptic of blasphemy after he argued a dripping crucifix was caused by faulty plumbing rather than divine intervention, leaving him facing a possible prison term. "Don't try to bring dark ages in India," he had warned in a TV discussion (AFP, 27 May, 2012). A Catholic school in Philippine banned Muslim hijab (head veil) in the Muslim majority Zamboanga (AFP, 05 Aug, 2012). The Christians are facing dilemma in the modern and real world. In August 2012, a weak and naked man was rescued from the sea off Perth in Australia after his boat capsized (The West Australian, 11 August, 2012). Surprisingly, the man's both palms were made in to a tower when he saw helicopter. Unlike Christians and Muslims, that is how Hindus worship. Was that the natural instinct or did he convert to Hinduism in dire emergency?

In early 2013, New Zealand lawmakers voted overwhelmingly in favour of a bill allowing gay marriage (Associated Press, 13 Mar, 2013). Usually, Kiwis follow Aussies but in this regard, Kiwis outsmarted Catholic leadership. Homosexuality was described by Psychiatrists as a transient phenomenon after puberty. Homosexuality is an alternative mean when people cannot get opposite sex partner. Also it is a way of preventing pregnancy. But now we see several homosexuals, both men and women being very vocal. Is this an aberration or natural phenomenon? An Australian senator compared homosexuality a step ahead of bestiality. The church insists that marriage means coupling between a man and a woman. Unfortunately, gays want their so called marriage in the church. This is a paradox. Gays should not worry about churches and conduct their marriages in so many other venues than to insist that churches change their policy. Another irony is that gay couple also want a child which is not possible without extra ordinary measures. Fortunately, IVF is a blessing for gays. In kindergartens, child care workers face a dilemma. When a child is brought to the centre by gay couples, it is very difficult to explain to other children where are the natural parents? Catholic countries like Ireland and Belgium ban abortions. But individuals from these countries travel to other European countries to have abortion. A dentist was denied abortion in Ireland and both the woman and foetus died. It was said in an Irish hospital that "it's a Catholic thing" (AAP, 9 April, 2013). So according to Catholics, instead of sacrificing the foetus, it is better to sacrifice both the mother and foetus.

ISLAM AND WOMEN

A man was charged with rape and murder of Jill Meagher, an Australian woman in Melbourne (ABC Sep 28, 2012). In US, Wisconsin lawmaker Roger Rivard said 'some girls rape easy' (The Ticket October 12, 2012). Did the Muslim cleric in Australia say that some women invite rape? People look at only one side immediately after the incident. It needs critical analysis to learn lessons. Mass hysteria and sympathy wave prevents critical analysis and learning. Was the woman alone and unsteady at 2 am on road? Why did the husband refuse to pick up her? Why did she refuse colleagues' offer to drop her? Of course any rational person will feel quite safe close to his or her home as happened in Jill's decision to go alone. The mechanized modern world lack respect for women. Video games, TV and pornography have made women's status in society worse than under Sharia law. Some criticize the Sharia law that marrying the rape victim as punishment disembowels and dehumanize women and also encourages rape. Blood money for murder equates life with money. The attacker agreed to marry a 14-year-old girl who was kidnapped and raped repeatedly for three days in Jordan to avoid going to jail. According to penal code Article 308 in conservative Muslim society rapists can walk free (AFP, 28 June, 2012**).** Prevalence of genital mutilation in Australia is in dispute. Professor Rane said that this practice had some degree of religious coercion. But Hanny Lightfoot-Klein, a leading international expert on female genital mutilation, categorically said that there was no link with Islam (ABC, 14 September, 2012). The so called female circumcision or genital mutilation aims to reduce the sensitivity and pleasure of women in the patriarchal society. There was nationwide call to implement death penalty for rape following the gang rape on 16 December 2012 in Delhi. Police culture in India often blames rape victims and refuses to file charges against accused attackers.

After living in few countries, the author formulated **two theories**. The first theory says about the political system of a country judged by a foreigner or a new comer. If a foreigner comes to know who the head of state is within one week after watching national news daily on TV, then that country must be having a monarch, dictator or an autocrat. On the other hand if the foreigner is still confused who the head of state is even after one week, that country has a vibrant democracy. Brunei and Malaysia under Dr. Mahathir were the examples of former. New Zealand and Australia are the examples of the latter. The second theory says about women's dress. How much women cover with their dress is inversely proportionate to their freedom in their society. Despite religious, cultural and geographical differences the theory holds. Women who are independent will have stylish dresses and less covered while the women who are submitted to men will cover most. A Muslim Man refused to stand for female magistrate claiming it was against his religion. That is, according to Islam men do not submit to women (7News Sydney, 20 May, 2013). Ultimately a compromise was reached that he would leave the court and re-enter after the magistrate has taken the seat. Thus, he didn't have to technically stand up for her.

The sexual harassment at David Jones was an eye opener. The victim was not a lower rank employee. She came out in public and exposed the perpetrator. The male ran away from Australia that too after obtaining large bonus from David Jones. The victim had several text messages in her phone from the male. The male was begging to excuse him and not ruin his life and career. Another lady came out accusing the same perpetrator of sexual harassment and vowed to join the case. When the case came up in court the perpetrator returned to Australia. The court requested both parties to reconcile out of court. Ultimately, the victim settled to accept only her legal costs from the perpetrator. The case which started with grandiose ended in average outcome. The other lady was left in limbo. Ironically the perpetrator was granted another job by another enterprise. Imagine what happens when the lower rank employees are subjected to sexual harassment? This is the reality for sexual harassment.

After the tragedy of Delhi rape, extreme suggestions were made how to punish rapists. Anna Hazare called to hang all rapists in public. Film maker Ram Gopal Verma called for the rapists to be "lynched and tortured to death instead of being just hung" (Island, 4 January, 2013). In Sharia law, stoning to death is a punishment for adultery, usually for women. Former Chief Justice of India, KG Balakrishnan warned that if rape entails capital punishment, then the chances of a rapist killing his victim will rise as it happened in the case of Jill Meagher. A leader of India's ruling Congress party Bikram SinghBrahma was slapped and beaten in public entirely by a mob of women after he entered a woman's house and raped her in the Bhutan border. Compared to other religions, Hindus worship women and goddesses. Those who allege that woman is a commodity among Muslims forget what the Christians did or do. Woman is an object owned by man in the patriarchal society for the Christian church which never considered the sexual satisfaction of woman. In Hinduism, there is 'Linga worship' which is really the depicting the male organ wedged in female organ. What that means is sex is considered as a miraculous phenomenon that unites the human beings with the gods. Of course pope will strongly deny that so that their faith is not shattered.

SYDNEY POLICE

According to a witness the man's hands were up and he looked at police with an expression of surprise when shot dead by Sydney cops. The justification for shooting the man to death by 3 plainclothes policemen was that Rodney Elkass pointed a gun. Even the coroner was surprised that Rodney a decent citizen was not a gangster (AAP,

3 December, 2012**).** A motorcyclist died in NSW after police chase but police were not charged for man slaughter. In Queensland there is a no chase policy to avoid unnecessary deaths. Sydney police chase led to the death of an innocent child as the driver slammed in to a child's pram. The driver was charged with manslaughter and convicted. A Collar Bomb girl waited for 10 hours when the best police in world contacted other countries how deal with it. Ultimately, it was only a hoax bomb. However, the brilliant Sydney police solved the mystery by good detective work and got the perpetrator arrested in US. How did they connect an e mail address the perpetrator left with computers and traced the man to US along his flight path? It was an excellent work by police which deserve commendation. He was convicted. Months later, a man held Parramatta, Sydney in lockdown for more than 12 hours while Sydney police did research. An ordinary man overwhelmed police with a hoax.

In March 2012, police officers shot dead Darren Neill in Sydney at Parramatta Westfield shopping complex after he had been on a violent rampage. There was concern whether the non lethal methods were tried before shooting dead. A Brazilian student was tasered 14 times before his death. He died after being tasered, repeatedly sprayed with capsicum spray, handcuffed and restrained (ABC, 16 October, 2012**).** Hand cuffed and already on ground but surrounded by 11 policemen torturing a boy??? These cops may be from RSPCA taught and trained that cruelty against animals is a sin but against humans is valour. Should the Sharia law be applied to police officers and they are subjected to multiple tasers so that they could feel the pain and torture?? The best experiment to check whether multiple taser will kill a human is to subject the 11 policemen to repeated taser and see whether any of them dies. None of the police were charged for manslaughter.

In December 2012, there was a neighbourhood dispute in Sydney. The police arrived and realized they were overwhelmed. They called Inspector Bryson for back up. In the presence of posse of police, Bryson was attacked from behind. He died later in the hospital (ABC, 7 December, 2012). How was it possible for the neighbours to attack the inspector surrounded by other policemen? There was a Facebook page mocking the dead as an insult to injury. Facebook refused to remove the offending page. The detective inspector was addressed as "Defective Anderson" (AAP, 11 December, 2012). This is the down side of freedom of expression and social media. Police were called to a Sydney leagues club to control violent fans. A fan was restrained by police but died. The coroner slammed the police that they ignited the situation and there was gross error of judgment (AAP, 24 January, 2013). No action was taken against the police. A mentally ill man was shot dead by police and police covered up the unreasonable action. An internal inquiry by the police found the shooting was justified. During the Police Integrity Commission hearing into the November 2009 shooting, the police woman who shot dead a mentally ill man admitted giving inaccurate information to investigators. In spite of several fatalities, there was no action against police as every time their action was justified. It appears that police is above law and they are law unto themselves. If police and defence forces are the last resort employment, society has to expect misconduct and corruption. Very few will be ready to die for the sake of Uncle Sam. Once they have joined as a last resort, frustration and fear leads to animal behaviour. Similarly corruption in police is inevitable.

In August 2012, nearly 40 striking workers at platinum mine were shot dead by South African police! It was worse that the Police chief who earlier warned of end to strike at any cost was a Black woman!! The playboy President Jacob Zuma said he was "shocked and dismayed at this senseless violence." But he refused to meet strikers!!! (AAP, August 17, 2012). It was worst that the South African police charged 250 miners for the shooting (by Police) deaths under an apartheid Law. Whenever white police shot dead any black, the others were charged for provoking the police. That was double jeopardy. After much outcry the cases were withdrawn and miners released. A similar incident happened in Sydney in 2010. Police laid a siege for gunman Nguyen. After the shooting and capture of the gunman, police accused Nguyen for shooting a policeman Bill Crews. Later, police admitted the policeman was shot dead by another policeman during the siege. What a clever police killing their own. What sort of training are they given? The gunman was charged for man slaughter and convicted. That means, whenever police made mistake, others would be charged similar to South African apartheid practice!

There was a bushman who was hiding for 6 years from police after committing crimes. When the police cornered him, the bushman Naden shot at Police and went in to hiding in bushes for Months. Can someone believe this story? But that was the fact. After 2 months of aerial and land search he was caught. During a parade in Sydney in March 2013, a teenager was subjected to police brutality. The police whacked his head against the ground and his blood was on the ground. Police told the onlooker who videoed the incident not to (7News Sydney, 6 March, 2013). What about police in other Australian states? A Brisbane policeman responded to a hold up call in May 2011. He was shot dead when he entered the premise. Was he wise enough to gate crash at a hold up without any precaution? Was that the training provided to policemen? Melbourne police had beaten 2 African teenage migrants, handcuffed and then falsely imprisoned them. Later police paid hundreds of thousands of dollars confidentially to settle a court case (ABC, 03June, 2012).

ALCOHOL, THE SOCIAL AND LEGAL DRUG

While the laws are harsh against other drugs calling them illicit drugs, alcohol is free for all. The social and legal drug only limits the age and the level intoxication while driving. There are so many studies and commission reports on drugs use but hardly few regarding the damage done by alcohol. This is a curse and menace in Aboriginal community which leads to self destruction. In the majority community, though the harm and damage is not well understood, the casualties are many. Aussies are known as boozers all over the world. Especially, when Aussies are abroad, they lose sight and resort to violence combined with alcohol. The Foreign Affairs ministry had been busy in many countries just because Aussies were drunk and stupid. They forget that other countries too have laws for the maintenance of harmony in society. The Aussies forget that though their country is big in land, it has very little significance in the world. People around the world may have heard that there is something called Australia but it makes little difference in their life. How are Australians known around the world? They are boozers, weather junkies and sports fanatics.

In Australia, most violence is related to alcohol. A senior magistrate warned that alcohol-fuelled violence has reached "epidemic proportions" (ABC, 25 February, 2013). 'A girl fell from balcony and dies during schoolies celebration' (Sydney Morning Herald, 23 November, 2012). What was common between this death and the death of a footballer in Las Vegas? Both happened during celebrations. Both were part of friends group. Will there be a lesson?

Another Aussie jumps in to sea and drowns in Australia. Another Aussie falls from a cliff in Australia and dies. A school leaver drowned in a resort pool in Fiji (AAP, 4 December, 2012). In April 2013, a groom died in a hotel. He was sliding on the railing of the stair case with the blessing of alcohol. The PRIME Suspect in all these cases is ALCOHOL. Two passengers were missing from a cruise (AAP, 10 May, 2013). CCTV showed the pair falling into the Tasman Sea, one immediately after the other. Was Alcohol a factor? An Australian national attacked the waiter in Serbia and has bitten off part of a waiter's finger (AFP 2 June, 2013). He was arrested by police. Is this another alcohol story? It was suggested that when sports stars go on holiday overseas, a chaperone or guardian angel must follow. That means sports stars are children or insane to look after themselves? The main culprit is again alcohol. If they think that their government can rescue them irrespective of their offence, they need to look at our dailies to realize how many Aussies are languishing in foreign jails. Further analysis will reveal that Australia has very little clout abroad. In future there will be additional levy for Australians while leaving airport to cover the costs of department of foreign affairs in consular support for the troubled Aussies abroad.

Drowning and shark attacks in one state are national news in Australia. Unfortunately, the sensational and thrilling shark attacks are few compared to the number of people drown each year. Most of the drowning is related to alcohol or lack of life vest. It is an irony that life guards' competition ends up in drowning. North Narrabeen Surf Life Saving Club organised a school holiday camp in NSW. Ironically, 2 females drowned since the organizers did not know that water would be released periodically from the dam (Yahoo!7, 25 September, 2012). Adventurers, mountain climbers and surfers do not wear life vest but government spends fortunes in their search even after the safe period is gone. They should be compelled to take insurance before adventures.

After a rugby match, a lady told on TV that the matches must be classified as morons play. It is not suitable for children because of vulgar language and violence. Where can we see classic boxing and wrestling? Watch Rugby matches and soccer games live!!! They deserve brain injuries and insanity for such displays. Compared to rugby and football, cricket has been a gentlemen's game. This does not mean football players and rugby stars are primarily uneducated thugs. The executive bodies of these games need to stick to zero tolerance. The Football League and Rugby League need to get tuition from Cricket Australia. Even barking at a player draws enough punishment as match fee fine or suspension from games. If the same intolerance is applied to football and rugby, we would not see such animal behaviours in the field. John Tomic, the father of tennis star was facing an assault charge in Spain (AAP May 29, 2013). He defended himself saying that was in self defence. The companion player had injuries on his face. Then he was banned from attending matches. That is how sports bodies should act to prevent violence in sports. Boxing causes punching syndrome due to repeated injuries to brain. Mohammad Ali is a pathetic example of such consequence. Tackle rugby is equally damaging but the fame encourages violent encounters. These stars will end up in later life with disabilities. There has been calls to ban boxing but tackle rugby needs equal attention.

Alan Jones won the Ernie award for the sexiest comment which included Christine Nixon in Melbourne (ABC, 27 September, 2012). The police chief of Victoria lied but later admitted that she was dining while Victoria was on fire. In her book she used the weakest and the last card, gender discrimination. There was sensation when an Australian mother was trying to hide her daughters born to an Italian. The legal circus went on for months. The Australian grand mothers said they were ready to go to jail for hiding the girls. Without legal knowledge and how Australian court system works the old ladies appeared as buffoons. Ultimately, justice prevailed. The mother kidnapped the girls from Italy. She should return to Italy to fight custody battle and NOT in Australia after kidnapping (ABC, 3October, 2012). On 12 June 2012 a Coroner ruled that a Dingo took away a baby 30 years ago because evidence was submitted Dingos killed human. Does it mean Dingo took away the particular baby? A fox in London entered bedroom and tore an infant's finger off after dragging him from his cot (AAP, Yahoo!7, 10 February, 2013). Keli Lane was found guilty of murdering her baby daughter 14 years ago (ABC, 13 December, 2010). But the baby's body was never recovered. Perhaps that was another Dingo case? Gilham was jailed for life in 2009 for murdering his parents in 1993. The New South Wales Court of Criminal Appeal set aside the verdict and acquitted him. He inherited the 1 Million assets of parents. The Uncle who challenged the verdict and nephew promised an appeal. Unfortunately within 1 month he died of heart attack. Then who killed the parents? Is this is another dingo case?

CORBY

Corby was caught in 2004 while attempting to import 4 kilograms of marijuana into Bali in her body board bag. The Australian federal police could have arrested her in Australia. But they chose not to do so but tipped off the Balinese authorities. She was sentenced to 20 years in jail. What a shame for Australian prime minister to request leniency from Indonesian President??? Australia struck a deal in return to release jailed young Indonesian people smugglers. Few months back prime minister said they were not minors. But later foreign minister Bob Carr said that the minors were being released as a goodwill (AFP, 25 April, 2012). Australia's human rights chief said Australia should apologise for jailing Indonesian children as adults after they came as crew on people smuggling boats. The Indonesian government said at least some fishermen had to be released before Corby could be pardoned. Australia thought they could bully Indonesia forgetting that Indonesia is totally an independent country and not the tail of US. A 34-year-old nurse from Melbourne was arrested in July 2012. She was charged with drug trafficking which carried a mandatory death penalty in a court in Kuala Lumpur. Is this another CORBY? Fortunately she was released and her companion was charged.

Two Indonesian children were locked up in an adult jail in Australia. Unfortunately, Australia has mishandled its foreign policy with Indonesia. The colonial and big brother mentality of Australia strained the relationship with Indonesia. A truly independent Indonesia responded in similar kind to the US protectorate Australia. Australia thought it could dictate terms to Indonesia. Unfortunately, Indonesia reacted indifferently to Australian requests. Australia decided unilaterally regarding refugees without any consultation with Indonesia. The Indonesians on people smuggling charges will lodge civil compensation suit (ABC, 11 September, 2012). Despite the Indonesians' proof of underage boat riders, Australia disregarded and treated them as adults with scientific proof. Unfortunately, Australia ate the humble pie and released the underage Indonesians to please the Indonesian government as a deal for pardon of the Australian drug smuggler Corby. The Indonesian president's reaction was very cold. He did not pardon but reduced the sentence of Corby. But nether government or Prime minister or Bob Carr did not utter a word regarding Chan and Sukumaran who are still on death row in Bali. This is despite Australia being against capital punishment. Again, is it racism?

SEPTEMBER 2001

The president of USA George Bush was talking of star wars during his election campaign in 2000. Unfortunately, the genius Osama Laden planned an attack on the infidels and crusaders using domestic missiles. Even Soviet Union could not have planned such a synchronized attack at 4 locations concurrently. The ordinary Osama and his supporters improvised domestic missiles for massive attacks. Even the security nerve centre of USA the Pentagon was not spared. Just planning such coordinated attack was not enough. It was text book precision attack at 4 locations with Osama's followers ready to die to teach a lesson to USA. How cleverly, the 4 groups obtained aviation training only on take off and hijacked the 4 planes to be used as missile during suicide attacks. Only one plane was shot down before reaching the target. That was the achievement of the mighty Americans who were living in fool's paradise thinking of star wars. Despite the atrocities committed against Muslims in Palestine for decades, the Yankees' notorious CIA had no idea of the scale of destruction that was to come. Segar identified himself with the hapless Palestinians. On the fateful day, Segar was delighted to watch the TV that the Satan was taught a lesson. Segar thought of taking off from work and to continue to watch the unfolding drama on BBC and CNN. If that was the feeling of a non Muslim, imagine how the Muslims would have felt enchanted at the massive attacks against USA.

The Americans had blindly supported Israel for the last 60 years despite several resolutions against the monster in the UN (Joe Klein, Road Map for Reform, TIME, 21 Feb, 2011). The barbaric country on earth could violate any law and roam without any consequence. There was even Nobel Prize to the key stakeholders but nothing changed on the ground for Palestinians. The US had gone round and round with Israel while giving empty promises to Palestinians. Remember, in 1990, Palestinians were asked to support war against Iraq for them to be rewarded later. Unfortunately, many years after the Iraq war, the Palestinians are still struggling to survive. That was the rallying point for Osama Laden in the Muslim world. Never ending atrocities committed by Israel against Palestinians led to the formation of Al Qaeda to launch Jihad or holy war against the Satan the US. Mass killings, repeated invasions, destruction of property, economic blockade, settlements and assassinations were carried out by Israel for the last 50 years with the unwavering support of US. Unable to target the junior Satan Israel, the Muslims targeted the major Satan US in their own soil. The Americans, while preaching democracy to Arafat, supported any dictator or monarch in the world. The Time magazine of 21 February 2011 precisely pointed out the hypocrisy of US.

That was a historic event to avenge the injustices inflicted upon the weak Palestinians by USA and Israel over the decades. Unfortunately, the crusaders and Satan failed to comprehend the reality. The psychopath Bush felt humiliated and powerless at the face of the massive attack. He whipped up emotions and the stupid Americans became prey to the mass hysteria at the loss of 3 thousand American lives. Had the 300 million Americans had a soul search and introspection, they would not have had the knee jerk reaction like idiots. Still, there was only one voice requesting the Yankees for soul searching **"why did this happen to us?"** Unfortunately, the solo voice was drowned in the madness led by Bush and blindly followed by millions of Americans. The single voice was none other than the editor of **'Washington Post'.** Had the Americans listened to this solitary voice, they could have averted many thousands of death of their own in the madness that followed. Pathetically, within days, even the Washington Post retracted its editorial unable to face the mass hysteria of foolish population.

The psychopath Bush drove all Americans to become crazy and anti Muslim in the madness. Had the American populace had introspection, Bush could not have led the Americans towards more deaths. In the melee, Bush started a crusade to replay the bible. **Jesus as promised returned to earth** and started destruction of Muslim world. Bush used the words 'crusade' in biblical terms which historically meant the war was against Muslims. He made the Muslims all over the world enemies of Americans. It was too late for him to correct his dictum few days later as damage had already been done. He called Muslim clerics and leading Muslims for consultation and assured that the war was against terrorism and not Muslims. That hardly changed the ground situation. Majority of Islamists are not terrorists and do not condone attacks by radical Islamists. Therefore equating all Islamists with terrorism is inviting further radicalisation (The Wall Street Journal, 29 May, 2013). His notorious slogan was borrowed from Nazis 'either you are with us or with enemies'.

The stupid Americans were so crazy, maniacal and hysterical. All what followed was barbaric, brutal and wide spread destruction of lives of Americans as well as innocent Muslims. The destruction of limbs and property were astronomical. Ironically, the stupid Americans were satisfied with the mad Bush's killing of many more Americans during avenge. Bush killed more Yankees than Osama and co could kill during September 2001. Osama became a hero over night not only for Muslims around the world but even for other minorities suffering oppression in other countries from majority or the might. According to Bush and many Americans, might was right. But what a heavy price they paid to establish their might and taking revenge against Osama and other Muslims around the world? Some might argue that even Washington Post retracted its editorial that Bush did not have an alternative than to channel the anger towards more self destruction and destruction of Muslim populace and territory.

The melancholic Bush ordered invasion of Afghanistan where Osama was supposed to be hiding. There is a saying in Tamil that the fool 'drilled the mountain and caught a rat'. This was exactly what mad Bush and idiotic Americans achieved by sacrificing further **5 thousand American lives**. What a brilliant idea from a genius like Bush. Unfortunately, the stupid Americans were hunting Osama but pardoned Bush who caused many more thousand deaths of Americans. The wise Americans would have hanged Bush for treason and causing more American deaths than Osama. In the madness, the Americans got even the name wrong calling for the head of Bin Laden. Their knowledge and wisdom about Arabs and their language was very limited. The word 'Bin' meant 'son of' and 'Binti' meant 'daughter of'. These two words are common for most Arabs and the Malays referring to sons and daughters. Unfortunately, Bush, CIA and Pentagon as well as millions of foolish Americans thought the villain's name was Bin Laden. If the American diplomatic core in Arab countries had corrected their government, Americans would have dropped the word Bin instead Osama. What actually it means is Osama, the son of Laden. Americans would have understood better if the context of Bin was put simply to their president George Bin Bush. Unfortunately the hysterical Bin Bush was hunting for Bin Laden. If the man Laden had 4 or 5 sons all of them would be Bin Ladens. Instead of calling Osama Laden, the whole world blindly followed the Bush to call Bin Laden, the villain of the crusaders.

There is a moral lesson from the 3 thousand years old epic Maha Bharatha that any wise person entering a cave or enemy line should have an exit strategy first before entering as explained by the death of Abiman, son of Arjun. Unfortunately, the valorous Abiman was killed as he did not know how to exit from the cordon of enemy after breaking in. This was exactly the history repeated when Bush and Americans went in to Afghanistan and Iraq. Even the presidential term of Bush was exhausted but the exit in Afghan was not visible at the end of the tunnel. In the Afghan war U.S. military lost **2,000 soldiers** in the 11 years while **1,190 more coalition troops** from other countries too died. More than **20,000 Afghan civilians** also died at the end of 2011. The U.S. led invasion of Iraq in 2003 to oust Saddam Hussein, costed the lives of nearly **4,500 U.S. troops** (Associated Press, 30 Sept, 2012**)**. At the end of war against Iraq in 1990, the 3 major key players George Bush Sr, Margaret Thatcher and Gorbachev lost their jobs but Saddam remained as leader of Iraq. The George Bush Jr was obsessed that the war his father started had not finished off Saddam. Junior thought September 2001 was a golden opportunity to finish what his father started. Unfortunately, the stupid Americans even re-elected the mad Bush in 2004. Fortunately, the idiotic Americans woke up from their slumber by 2006. The stupid

Americans realized now that the wars in Iraq and Afghan had killed more Americans than in September 2001. Wide spread protests and picketing started demanding the US troops to come home. But that was too little too late. There were no weapons of mass destruction. It was only a story created by psychopath Bush. Lately the definition of weapon of mass destruction has been modified by US to suit the reason given for invasion of Iraq. In May 2013, the Boston bomber was charged with "using and conspiring to use a **weapon of mass destruction (WMD)** against persons and property." But whatever weapons used by US are not WMD. At the Leveson inquiry Tony Blair admitted that he made several calls to Rubert Murdock in the run up to Iraq invasion. An intruder how appropriately shouted that Blair was a war criminal.

George Bush and Dick Cheney were accused of "war crimes, plunder and murder" by an American soldier injured in Iraq war. Mr Young spoke on behalf of the 4,488 US soldiers and marines who have died in the war. He wrote on behalf of the countless Iraqis wounded and 1 million Iraqis dead. He accused that Bush and Cheney dodged the draft in Vietnam. His final message was "My life is coming to an end. I hope you will be put on trial. You, Mr. Bush, make much pretence of being a Christian. But isn't lying a sin? Isn't murder a sin?"(The West Australian, March 22, 2013**)**. Anyway, killing in the name of Jesus is not a sin. In 2013, US state secretary Kerry aptly expressed that Americans had a right to be stupid and disconnected (Reuters, 27 Feb, 2013**)**. That was exactly what Americans did following Bush from 2001 until 2006. Segar was an admirer of Castro and Gaddafi from childhood. After the war in 1990, Segar admired even Saddam. These leaders would have been cruel dictators but they stood up against the Satan America. Later on even Venezuelan President Hugo Chavez who died in March 2013 was admired. The NATO forces in Afghanistan needed a supply route across Pakistan which was closed following drone attack and civilian deaths. Pakistan military threatened and warned US against drone attacks at the beginning. But later, drone attacks became periodical without any response from Pakistan. Similarly civilian deaths became periodical in Afghanistan. President Karzai also threatened and warned but attacks were repeated. When the Yankees leave Afghanistan, Karzai has to run behind US for his safety. He has presided over the deaths of thousands of innocent civilians. The US puppet will not have any safe place other than US. In April 2012, the biggest coordinated attack on the Afghan capital had shaken NATO troops. That was during the royal farce when Prince Harry was co-pilot gunner. Former foreign minister Alexander Downer said Karzai was "urbane". Former commander of Australian forces in Afghanistan said that for political reasons Aussie soldiers were fighting a futile war in Afghan.

Following a series of anti-American statements by Afghan President Hamid Karzai, the top U.S. commander in Afghanistan warned his troops to be ready for increased violence (Associated Press, 15 March, 2013). There were 4 US generals in Afghanistan since 2008: Gen. David McKiernan, Gen. Stanley McChrystal, Gen. David Petraeus and Gen. John Allen. Australian defence force chief David Hurley admitted that military intervention alone could not solve Afghanistan's problems but development and diplomatic efforts (ABC, 21 Jan, 2013). Retired Major General John Cantwell admitted very frankly "It's not worth an Australian life. **Show me one thing in Afghanistan that is better because we've sacrificed any one of the 38** who have so far died there."(The Daily Telegraph, 17April, 2012). The wisdom was too little too late. Imagine the pain of the 38 families. Unfortunately, while in the position, these generals do not caution the politicians. In November 2012 while Australian troops were training in Afghanistan a civilian teenager was killed (AAP November 3, 2012). Was it callous disregard for civilians and natives or utter incompetence? In March 2013 Australian soldiers killed two Afghan children (Associated Press, 03 March, 2013). Has any soldier been punished for the civilians' death? Is the Muslim cleric wrong in sending condolence letters to war widows in Australia? A Brave woman was arguing with London attackers who killed a soldier in London (Associated Press, 25 May 2013). The attacker's logic was that the victim killed Muslim women and children in Iraq and Afghanistan. Therefore, the soldier is a legitimate target. In April 2012, to have maximum political impact during election in 2013, Prime Minister Julia Gillard announced that Australian troops would be coming home from Afghanistan a year earlier than planned. Unfortunately, within 24 hours, on the advice of the master, the US, in an apparent U-turn Australia vowed to keep combat troops in Afghanistan through 2014. "Australia is looking increasingly silly for insisting it will stay the course in Afghanistan" said Greens leader Christine Milne (ABC, 5 October, 2012). Australia recruited child soldiers till 1970 to be mercenaries for the Americans' wars. Australia never had a war. Australian soldiers were only mercenaries for UK until World War 2. Thereafter Australia was forced to send mercenaries for the wars of Americans. Most countries have cut and run to save their lives with some form of camouflage. Italian prime minister, as his country pulled out its troops, emphasised not to abandon Afghanistan (Associated Press, 4 Nov, 2012). Five Australian troops were killed in an "insider attack" by an Afghan solider in August 2012. That was the worst since Vietnam War. The Aussie soldiers fired at the rogue Afghan but still he escaped after killing 3 and wounding 2. What a great achievement! So, one Afghan gunman could outsmart several Aussie soldiers? Army Gen. Martin Dempsey of US admitted that resilient Taliban would be a threat in Afghanistan even after US pulled its forces by end of 2014. So, what have they achieved in 12 years than sacrificing many American lives (Associated Press, 8 April, 2013)?

Despite tribal traditions that prohibit women from speaking to strangers, an Afghan woman described what happened sometime before dawn on March 11 (Associated Press, 17 May 2012). An American soldier wearing a helmet equipped with a flashlight was on rampage. He burst into her mud home while everyone was asleep. He killed her husband, punched her 7 year-old son and put a pistol into the mouth of his baby brother. A man said when he returned home from a trip the morning after the attack he found 11 members of his family dead and their bodies were partially burned. Even recently the US lost 6 personnel including two American soldiers and four American civilian contractors when a suicide bomb exploded killing 15 people (Associated Press, 17 May, 2013). 'NATO and US troops will withdraw from Afghan by end of 2014' is again a farce. The US bases are needed to protect the US puppets and stooges. The US puppet Karzai has no moral right to enter in to any long term agreement with the Satan. Afkhan is not a private property of Karzai (Associated Press, 9 May, 2013). If it is said that there will be only 9 bases the actual bases will be more. In Iraq, the US troops withdrew but a fortified base with high rise neo-Berlin wall remains. Without a referendum, no Afghan can allow US bases. It appears US has learnt a good lesson after the terrible experiences in Iraq and Afkhan. Obama was reluctant to be involved on the ground in Libya. Now, the Syrian conflict is going on for months but US which burnt its feet is waiting and waiting (Reuters, 28 April, 2013). Mad Bush started the Crusade which has no light at the end of the tunnel. Korea and Vietnam lessons were forgotten by Bush. The US generals are pessimistic of the outcome if US is involved in Syria.

Julia Gillard justified the involvement in Afghanistan by referring to Bali bombing of Aussies. What a convenient amnesia? Bali bombing was in October 2002 in retaliation for the involvement of Aussies in Afghanistan since 2001. Independent MP Andrew Wilkie said that politicians had blood on their hands for allowing Australian troops to remain in Afghanistan. Liberal backbencher Mal Washer believed that Australia was only involved in the conflict "to appease the Americans" (AFP, 30 Aug, 2012). This is the only issue Liberal Opposition and Labour Government are united at. John Howard not only lost election of his Government but also his own seat after 30 years in 2008. One of the reasons was the war in Iraq and Afghanistan. Many conscientious Aussies protested on streets and showed the discontent at election. Unfortunately, the Labour also could not go against the master, the US. Remember Kevin Rudd made a military salute to US president. When George Bush declared war against Muslims, the Aussie office boy and British office assistant did not have a choice than joining the boss. The wars in Korea and Vietnam have not taught any lesson to the dependant country called Australia. Australia is NOT an independent country but a US protectorate. Unfortunately, the defence chiefs, as expected follow the order of political masters. They wait for retirement to voice their anger and opposition to Iraq and Afghanistan wars. If the defence chiefs had been outspoken while in service like some US defence commanders, Australia could have avoided the wars in Iraq and Afghanistan. Only the Green party was against any involvement in Afghanistan and said it was wrong to be there in the first place.

IRONY

The CIA recruited Pakistani surgeon to use a fake hepatitis B vaccination campaign to obtain DNA samples of Osama Laden's family (AFP, 24 May, 2012). Ultimately, CIA zeroed on Osama Laden. Americans continue to hold Afghan detainees without a trial though the main American run prison was handed over to Afghan (Associated Press, 10 Sep, 2012). Sovereignty of Iraq and Afghan are farce. US have a fort in Iraq with a high wall. The Berlin wall was destroyed in 1990 but the **US reinvented the wheel with walls in Iraq and Palestine.** President Karzai banned Afghan security forces from requesting international airstrikes on residential areas following civilian deaths though government troops relied heavily on foreign air power to give them an advantage against Taliban (Associated Press, 3 Mar, 2013). The Afghan regime could collapse upon NATO's withdrawal though 11 years have lapsed (AFP, 9 October, 2012). An Israeli soldier who shot dead a Palestinian mother and daughter waving a white flag during the 2009 offensive in the Gaza Strip was sentenced to 45 days in prison instead of a manslaughter conviction and a 20 year imprisonment (AAP, 13 August, 2012). Musharaf of Pakistan was accorded royal treatment just to support the Afghan war. Musharaf, a criminal, coup leader and dictator was given red carpet welcome in the House of Lords in London. That was a stark irony for a dictator instead of being paraded before international criminal court.

A photo appeared depicting US soldiers urinating on the bodies of dead Taliban fighters in Afghanistan. That was the extreme behaviour of the forces of Satan. The soldiers would face court martial and as usual the punishment would be only symbolic (AFP, September 25,

2012). Then is it wrong if Muslim clerics send sarcastic letters to the widows of Aussie veterans? Cuba's Castro stepped down due to his cancer. Then, the state secretary of US master, Condoleezza Rice urged the Cubans to rise up against the regime. Then is it wrong if Muslim clerics send sarcastic letters to the widows of Aussie veterans'? Khalid MD Sayed was tried in Gitmo, 10 years after 9/11. He was in Gitmo for 6 years though Obama signed closure of Gitmo 3 years ago. Bush-Cherny duo reinvented what Soviet Union and Chinese communist party did few decades ago. It was a full circle that US resorted to extra ordinary measures to deal with suspects. The Soviet Union and Chinese were telling the same theme that extra ordinary situation necessitated extra ordinary measures. Water boarding was widely used though it was torture. Human Rights Watch said that there were abuses of prisoners while they were held in US led detention centres in US or its interrogation centres in Pakistan, Morocco, Thailand and Sudan (Island, 6 Sept, 2012). That was nothing strange for US which committed genocide and ecocide with Orange agent in Vietnam. Nearly 400 thousand Vietnamese died of Dioxin (Associated Press, 7 Aug, 2012). It was the 'napalm girl' photo from Vietnam that changed the course of war. The concrete cross of the 1966 battle of Long Tan where 18 Australians were killed and 24 were wounded was a symbol of disgrace. The Aussies who denied atrocities and crimes venerated the cross after 46 years. Former state secretary Madeleine Albright was questioned how could half a million Iraqi children were allowed to die due to US economic sanctions. The moron's reply shocked the journalists when she replied 'It was worth the price!' It was nothing new after killing nearly 4 million Vietnamese in the 1970s. Nagasaki and Korea were other examples of crimes against humanity by US. Egypt's dictator Hosni Mubarak was sentenced to life but his 2 sons were cleared. Compare this to the massacre of Gadhafi and hanging of Saddam by kangaroo court.

This is the double standard of US. In September, 2012 American ambassador to Libya, Chris Stevens, and three officials were killed in the eastern city of Benghazi, when a mob attacked the US consulate during protest against a film made by an Israeli-American who described Islam as a "cancer" and depicted the Prophet Mohammed sleeping with women (AFP, 12 September, 2012).

REFUGEES

A boat with 200 asylum seekers sent distress signal on Tuesday 18 June 2012 between Australia and Indonesia. Next day Wednesday Australian plane spotted the boat but did nothing. Only when the boat capsized on Thursday Australian plane and customs went to help. By the time, 90 people drowned. The Green party leader Christine Milne asked why no action was taken before the boat capsized? In Dec 2010, when a boat crashed near X Mas island many died. Did Australian customs wait until the tragedy took place? Why was the prime minister blaming Tony Abbot for asylum bill defeat? Julia should ask the government partners Green to support Malaysia solution than blaming Abbot. Sarah Hanson the Green MP said Australia should open doors to asylum seekers in a humane way. Before 2010 election the only person who advocated liberal Asylum policy without playing to the gallery was Bob Brown, Green leader. Bob Brown pressed with Carbon Tax, put Labour in trouble and then retired. After refusing for 2 years, PM Julia Gillard agreed on 13 August 2012 to restore John Howard's Pacific solution when Angus Houston panel recommended. This panel was appointed after Greens and Liberals refused Malaysia solution and the boats kept flooding. The panel was a face saver for Julia's about turn after so much blood in her hands. All those who opposed the panel recommendations and the bill hurried in 48 hours were whites from Green Party and Uniting church. Ironically, none of the minorities objected to the express bill.

Former Ambassador to Indonesia Tony Kevin said Australian navy instead of giving second class treatments to boat people should do more to save refugees' lives. Australian navy dodged at least on 4 occasions. The offshore processing of refugees was condemned by Greens, Uniting church and former prime minister Malcolm Fraser. He said In August 2012 that the offshore processing of refugees was RACIST policy. On 25th March 2013, customs boat followed a refugee boat and waited until it capsized. This resulted in the death of a mother and child. Asylum seekers who suffered trauma and psychological damage in detention centres would start legal action which could result in multi-million dollar compensation payouts by government. The treatment of refugees by Australian government is not much different from the inhuman treatment meted out to refugees including whipping by Malaysia. Though there is no physical punishment, the refugees undergo indirect psychological abuse by immigration department of Australia. They are treated almost par with cattle. Even children have been mistreated. Though the theory is different, the practice of immigration department has not changed much from the Howard era.

THE AUTHOR

The year 1958 was remarkable for Segar. He had cleaned his right ear with a stick which resulted in ear discharge and fever and his body went in to spasms from time to time. The doctors at the northern town hospital of Sri Lanka diagnosed Tetanus and transferred the child to the general hospital in the northern city. The treatment of Tetanus was not very successful in those days. However, after 3 weeks of hospital stay and struggle Segar was discharged from hospital. When he was 8 years old his teachers noticed Segar's ability to debate with eloquence. He was upstaged on the foundation day celebration with an oration. This gave Segar the confidence to become very vocal. Segar was leading his friends through his articulation. While being an advocate for Tamil language, Segar was a devoted Hindu in the foot steps of his mother. But suddenly his attitude changed. At the age of 13 Segar stumbled across a small book which narrated briefly the life story of Swami Vivekananda, a radical Hindu monk. Segar read more of the monk's preaching. This changed the thoughts and life of Segar. From being a traditional Hindu, Segar transitioned in to a radical and realized that non conformity would be his style of life. He learnt not to submit but defend the vulnerable and feeble. He learnt from his mother that weak side or person need not surrender. As long as nothing wrong or immoral has been committed, he wanted to exercise his freedom and choice to the maximum though it may not conform to the orthodox values and behaviour. He started writing essays, delivering speeches and winning prizes in the school. Once he won gold medal in the all island oratory competition. This was the time Segar decided that he would do medicine and serve the local people. The teachers preferred him to do Arts subjects because of Segar's talent in oratory and writing. Segar failed miserably in the school cricket. But he was leading teams in soft ball cricket. Segar failed in soccer because he was not good at dodging the ball. In athletics Segar was average. Thus Segar achieved nothing in sports or physical activity. His only strength was his foul mouth.

Segar's friends started a manuscript monthly magazine. At the age of 14-15 those magazines were routinely filled with Segar's articles and verses. The rest was done by an artistic friend and two other friends who were the editors. Few months later, a rival magazine was released against the gang of four. Segar, instead of encouraging, became so jealous and decided to challenge. Single handed Segar released a magazine, criticising many aspects of the rival magazine. Segar did not want another or rival leader to express ideas. In 1968, the Hindu temple in the hills of the campus in the central Sri Lanka was inaugurated. Segar and another friend of Segar were sent to the temple as representatives of the school. In the temple when an opportunity was given to make a brief comment, Segar inappropriately raised the morality of running a raffle among school students by the education department. That was a silly statement at a Hindu temple abusing the forum. The white German Swamy and Tamil leader GG Ponnambalam were the special guests.

Segar refused to buy the raffle ticket being sold in schools by education department. The principal summoned him. Segar argued that even raffle was based on gambling. Therefore he would not buy as smoking, drinking and gambling were taboos and non-negotiable. Segar's school was popular for discipline where white trouser and white shirt was the uniform. Once in 1970, he wore a red and blue trouser and shirt which were tied and dyed. Segar bought the crimson red dye and blue dye. He tied certain parts and dipped the white dress in the dyes. The trouser and shirt looked mosaic in red and blue on white background. This created a stir in the school and Segar was summoned by the deputy principal. The stupid Segar argued that though the school uniform dress was advocated to maintain equality among students there was inequality in the quality and price of the cloth of the uniform. He was instructed to remain inside the class and not to venture out. He was reprimanded not to wear the colourful dress again. The same year Segar met principal Raj and demanded that the high school annual dinner speeches should be in Tamil instead of English. He dropped a veil threat that the dinner could be boycotted if English speeches went ahead as usual. The principal suggested a compromise that there would be a Tamil speech in addition to English. Segar responded that he would think about it and return after discussing with his friends. Later Segar agreed for the compromise to incorporate both languages at the dinner. Many thought Segar bargained just because he wanted deliver a speech. Fortunately, Segar wrote the speech and got it delivered through proxy. There were reversed roles for Segar and the school principal in 1971. Segar wanted to sit for the university entrance exam for the second time from the school while studying at home. The principal had a sweet revenge. He insisted that nobody would be allowed to sit for the exam without further attendance at school. However, he told Segar to come and meet him after one week to know his final decision. The deputy principal offered to intervene on behalf of Segar. But a week later, the principal consented for Segar to sit for the exam through the school.

MEDICAL COLLEGE

Segar had to be away from home for the first time to pursue medical studies at the university in central Sri Lanka. The so called ragging to make the fresh students become more sociable was very often sadistic and at times sexually explicit. Very often the senior students who inflicted physical and sexual abuse on fresh students were themselves abused earlier. This goes on in a vicious cycle perpetuated year after year. Unless serious bodily harm took place most of the ragging went unnoticed and accepted as standard civilized process. There was a dental student Yoga who became the victim instead of his brother in law judge. After watching the humiliation, intimidation and watering from the bucket, Segar salvaged Yoga though his friends were dismayed. Segar offered warm tea and dispatched Yoga. Pathirana was a medical student running in panic to avoid the ragging. Segar once escorted him to the bus stand to escape home. Unfortunately, the following year, Segar noticed that Pathirana was involved in ragging his juniors. The residential facility made the new students more vulnerable. Lack of forthcoming witness made any complain irrelevant.

HOME TOWN

Segar was very much attracted by the selfless service of catholic priests especially among the so called low caste Tamils. Just before starting work, Segar had a catholic cassock stitched for him. It was an insult to Catholic priests and laughable but Segar was fascinated by the dress and selfless work of Catholic priests. Segar had a photo in the catholic dress. But his mother being worried whether that could be the beginning of conversion from being Hindu to a Catholic burnt the cassock. Segar was too happy to work in the hospital in his home town. Most people were known to him and Segar helped them day and night though he was paid by the government for limited hours only. This was the time Segar was performing autopsies in his home town and appeared in the magistrate court many times. In one case the entire family of 7 including 2 children were shot dead in the northern town. The suspects had a family feud with another. One week prior to the incident, several dogs in the vicinity were poisoned to death. The people did not take much notice. Later, with hindsight the relatives realized that there was a danger signal when the dogs died but was missed. The suspects had used shot guns and killed the entire family sleeping in one house. Only the family head Narayan survived. Few months later, when Segar was on holiday in Brunei, the Strait Times daily of Singapore carried news that 3 people were shot dead in Northern Sri Lanka. That was the revenge for the previous shooting. The suspects were being transported from Magistrate's court to prison by bus with escort. When the bus stopped at a station at mid point, a gang got in to the bus and shot dead the suspects.

Segar's ex-classmate Kuru managed to bring to the northern district the comedian, politician and journalist Cho from Chennai. The mayor refused to be the chief guest to avoid any controversy. The commissioner of the municipality also refused to be associated with a controversial politician of Chennai. Fortunately, the mayor changed his mind and consented to be the chief guest. There was a massive crowd at the function hall in the northern district where Cho spoke and answered questions. This was largely the combined effort of Kuru and Segar. While Segar was delivering the welcome address where city mayor was the chief guest and Cho was the guest of honour, the crowd became out of control. There was an entry donation ticket but ultimately the crowd pushed their way in to the hall and perimeter.

Segar and Kuru managed to organize another function in the northern town where Cho was comical and assertive. The doctors from the hospital of northern town were invited to Segar's home for an audience with Cho. Few days later Segar was confronted with massive bills of entertainment tax from the city council as well as the secretary of the town council where the two functions were held respectively. Segar met the mayor and commissioner of the municipality and sought the influence of mayor saying that the ticketing system failed due to massive crowds and there was actually a loss. The mayor who had been the chief guest was embarrassed that Segar was caught with tax bill. After negotiation, mayor and commissioner waived the tax. Similarly Segar met the secretary of the town council who was actually confronted at the function demanding that he bought a donation ticket. Segar explained the circumstances that the purpose was to cover the expenses but at the ground level everything was out of control. The tax was waived.

In the hospital in northern town, Segar was actively involved in sterilization surgery. Another lady doctor was also very much involved. Males or females with 2 or more children were sterilized as a permanent solution to poverty and over population with the consent of the spouse. In the meantime, methods to postpone pregnancy were promoted too. Segar delivered several lectures on planned parent hood to teachers, school leavers and health volunteers. Segar strongly believed that quality of people was more important than quantity. Unfortunately, not everyone agreed where the number of heads mattered most. During a farewell speech in

1984, Segar made public pronouncement on the stage. Segar said "the number is not important but the strength of each individual. Israel could outsmart several Arab countries and Japan was leading world economy with minimum numbers".

After the farewell speech at the hospital, Segar joined a private clinic nearby. The doctor who was working there broke away and started his own clinic. The practice of Dr Selva was most inhumane. Anyone vulnerable would be admitted to the clinic and intravenous fluids would be pumped. Though it was a clinic and not hospital few beds served the purpose. Most of the time those patients did not need any injection or intravenous fluids. It was very unethical and inhumane business centred only on money. After Selva started his own clinic, the previous clinic needed a doctor. This was the time Segar was transferred from the hospital of his hometown. Segar agreed to work in the private clinic for few months. The owner of the clinic indirectly tried to influence Segar to milk in more money from patients than worrying about patients' welfare. Segar had been working for government where he was paid a fixed salary and monetary concerns did not influence the ethical practice. More so because he was working in his home town day and night without any extra pay. In private medical clinics the sick and wounded were forced to pay money unnecessarily. Segar realized that medicine was not a business and he could not commercialize medicine. After 3 months Segar quit the private clinic and decided never again to practice medicine in private.

Several months later Selva was caught by his wife while he was sleeping with his sister in law. He had given injections to his wife to sleep and then started an affair with his sister in law. Unfortunately his family itself publicised the news and it became the talk of the town. Much to the amusement of the town, Selva and his sister in law wanted to get married. Another Dr Myl was caught in the northern town hospital while sexually abusing a mental patient. Before this, Dr M had animosity against a nurse Mahes. It was this nurse who called Dr M's wife who was admitted for child birth and exposed the doctor. When Segar was working in the hospital in the northern city Dr Anton from Anuradhapura hospital visited the north during holidays. He used to boast that in their hospital any woman who sought abortion had to sleep with every doctor before surgery. Further, in the same district any woman who wanted divorce had to pay not only the fee but also sleep with the lawyer. When Segar was once in the Anuradhapura hospital for one day when he was transferred from north, a doctor came and asked Dr Thanga that they wanted to use his room for sexual activities.

Segar did not want to work away from home but went to Saudi Arabia for work. The Arabs were cordial though few were uncivilized and rude. The Muslim chief told Segar that he could use the Islamic greeting "Asalamu Alaikum". However, he was told that he could not visit Mecca the holy city unless he converted to Islam. Saudi was rich but corrupted as well. The industry or business licences were issued to locals only. But the locals will sell the licence to foreigners. Thus the businesses became foreign owned. Alcohol was prohibited but during weekend Muslims could take 7 minutes flight to neighbouring Bahrain for alcohol and sex. The Filipino nurses were known to have prostituted for 500 Riyals (1984/1985). The Thai used to cut apples, potato and bread and soaked in water for few days underground to ferment so they could have their own brew. The police would make raids from time to time and excavate the brew from hiding places. The Thai were also showing porn films and charging a fare from audience. Several Thai workers were interested in boosting the male organ at their bottom so that they could seduce rich women. It was a modified circumcision to increase the circumference and increase friction so that the woman experiences more pleasure. Thais called this Tri Star Benz where the excess skin, instead of being removed, just split in to 3 petals and left behind. Another means was to insert beads on the surface of the skin which again gave the same effect. Few had both, tri star Benz modification as well as bead insertion. At the request, Segar performed the surgery for few Thais who would resort to any means to enhance their potency. Their practice was crude and with no antiseptic done by few quacks, usually from Philippines. After few months Segar returned to Sri Lanka and started to work in his home town again.

ETHICAL OR NOT?

Segar followed the rules and regulations during his work except on few occasions in northern town in Sri Lanka. Segar had zero tolerance for alcohol. Whenever Dr Myl was seen drunk in the hospital, Segar commandeered the ambulance and dropped Dr M in his home. Occasionally drunk visitors created pandemonium in the hospital. Segar got the drunken person tied to a pillar for others to watch. Once Segar called police and handed over such a person while under the influence of alcohol just to avoid any allegation of abuse by Segar. There was a young lad who threatened the staff and Segar was notified. The boy was tied to a post and later released on the request by relatives. Since most doctors were females, it was Segar who had to maintain discipline in the hospital. Segar believed that charging in court of law a person who failed in committing suicide was double blow and did not give an opportunity for the survived individual a second chance. The survivor, instead of getting more surveillance and active support, had to face legal battle or end up in prison. That is the best recipe for another attempt at suicide. A friend, Sri requested Segar to unofficially visit his sick mother in their home. In addition to being personal friend, they have been family friends as well. The elderly lady who survived breast cancer 10 years ago was suffering so much not only with recurrence of cancer but also with wide spread metastasis. She was in excruciating pain with no meals except some liquid. Segar felt beyond any hope and the eldest son refused to bring the patient to hospital for relief of pain. In that circumstance nobody would dispute that the patient has come to an end. After talking to the son, Segar had to make a critical decision. Segar asked himself whether there would be any monetary gain by the death of the patient to anyone including the patient's family as well as the doctor. Segar was convinced beyond any doubt that there were no such possibilities. Segar asked himself whether he would perform the same to his mother had she been terminally ill and the answer was definite affirmative. The son and Segar decided that the patient needed some relief from the pain and suffering. The son agreed that he was becoming sick watching his beloved mother suffering so much.

Segar pronounced his plan of action to the son of patient. Though, appeared cruel to terminate the life of the suffering patient, Segar and the son of patient agreed that it was the reasonable thing to do. Segar and the patient's son visited a pharmacy and bought 2 vials of Diazepam and a 5 cc syringe without any prescription. No records were maintained. The only witness for Segar was the son of the patient who was Segar's friend as well. In the home of the patient, Segar again asked the son whether he wanted his mother to die peacefully. The son was not wavering. Segar injected the medicine very fast and the patient's breathing stopped immediately as expected. This medicine is used in fits and also to induce sleep. The tablet is used as tranquilizer in anxiety. The worst side effect of the injection was respiratory arrest especially if not given very slowly. Segar and the son of the patient had a sigh of relief. Another way to bring about the same outcome was to inject massive doses of pain killer or inject potassium chloride in to the vein. Segar believed that at least few doctors practised disguised euthanasia. He also believed in pro-choice than the so called pro-life advocacy.

Under any circumstance **Euthanasia** or mercy killing was illegal and unethical in Sri Lanka. The upper house in New South Wales voted down voluntary euthanasia bill. Only 13 voted in favour and 23 voted against (ABC, 23 May, 2013). The green's member proposed to allow terminally ill people to request assistance to die. Is this a catholic thing? An elderly councillor in UK compared disabled children to deformed lambs that need to be culled (The West Australian, 14 May, 2013). His theory was based on economics. He said whether children with disabilities should live or not depended on the cost. There is a risk that people with disabilities may become victim of euthanasia. The religious leaders interfere in all aspects of life depriving the individual the right to determine. Whether it was abortion or mercy killing, the religious leaders influence politicians from acting. The anti abortion group, mostly radical Catholics or Muslims oppose abortion. Thus the individual loses the right to decide his or her future. On the other hand, excessive medicalization of birth and death deprive humane life. Perpetuating the life of a brain dead person with the help of machines is ridiculous. Birth and death are natural phenomena. At one stage death has to be accepted and only relief is provided to avoid any suffering. Just because of the tale of the suffering of Jesus at cross (or stake as Jehovah's claim), others need not go through same.

In the early times of medical history, before using cruel medicines, the question was asked whether the physician would use the same medicine on himself. Segar was determined that euthanasia was the appropriate treatment for him in terminal illness than connecting so many cables, electrodes and tubes to machines and human body to perpetuate life for a brief period. There are several reasons why euthanasia could not be legalized. Certainly the religious monarch Pope would not endorse. Even in non Catholic countries, politicians are controlled by religious leaders. The holy pro-life lobby is very powerful irrespective of the religion. The abortion law requires at least 2 medical persons to attest that abortion was in the best interest of the pregnant mother. This is to prevent commercialization of abortion by medical person. Similarly euthanasia can be facilitated legally. Segar gave advance medical directive to his family. If Segar is conscious and capable of making decisions, then Segar will assert himself and make decision. The medical directive is to be implemented if Segar is unconscious or unable to make decision. If Segar is unconscious for 48 hours, then he wants all cables, electrodes, tubes and machines to be removed from his body. He does not believe in cremation or funeral. He wants to donate heart, kidney, liver and cornea. He wants his cadaver to be donated to the medical school of Western Sydney University.

Karu was Segar's very close classmate for few years. The shrewd and smart Karu was working in 2 departments at the same time. He joined agriculture department after leaving from teaching. While employed in agriculture department he was given an official motor cycle. That was taken away by someone. Unfortunately, Karu had to return the motorbike or pay the price. Karu left agriculture department and rejoined teaching. He wanted medical certificate to fill the gaps. Segar issued for one month with the diagnosis of anxiety. This was extended up to 3 months. Then, Segar threatened Karu that he should make up his mind and stay with one job or else Segar would notify both education department and agriculture department. Ultimately, Karu stayed with education department

Once, Segar visited the northern city general hospital where Karu's wife was in coma during her first pregnancy following fits. That was eclampsia or hypertensive toxaemia of pregnancy and the patient recovered after a live baby was delivered through a caesarean. One year later Karu brought his wife to the northern town hospital to be seen by Segar. She was advised not to get pregnant for 2 years because of eclampsia during first pregnancy and the caesarean. Now she had become pregnant at the end of one year and in addition she was an asthmatic patient who required nebulisation very often. Segar calculated the period of pregnancy and was convinced it was only 11 weeks. Karu requested Segar to perform abortion in the interest of his wife as well as the one year old child. Segar had observed how Karu's wife narrowly escaped death during first pregnancy. Without any hesitation, Segar agreed to perform abortion. She was taken to the obstetric ward and Segar told midwife that the patient was having bleeding on and off without any regular menses. The patient was given pain killer in to the vein very slowly. Unusually, Karu was allowed to be the witness during the procedure though in those days and in those territories males were not allowed during child birth or any gynaecological procedure. That was to reassure the patient and to convince the midwife that there was nothing suspicious. Segar performed the abortion and was sure nothing was left behind. After a brief stay and ensuring there was no more bleeding, Karu and his wife were allowed to leave the hospital. Karu profusely thanked Segar for understanding the circumstance without any fuss of legality or formality as no record was kept. Unfortunately, few years later, when Segar returned to country from abroad, learnt from Karu that his wife died one year after the abortion due to uncontrolled asthma.

In a similar circumstance, Segar's friend and family friend Nesan, brought his wife to the northern town hospital. She had a caesarean one year ago but had become pregnant again despite the medical advice to the contrary. Further, both husband and wife did not want another child. Segar readily agreed to perform abortion and it was done in the same hospital and the couple left hospital very happy without any complication soon afterwards. Unfortunately, few months later there was a misunderstanding due to some other social problem and the husband and wife were living separately. Segar wanted to reconcile the couple and intervened after both individuals consented. When Segar and another friend went with Nesan's wife to Nesan's house as agreed by both parties for reconciliation talk, Nesan could not resist his mother and absconded. Segar and friend were very disappointed that Nesan betrayed so badly. Nesan's wife repeatedly asserted that her prediction was right and Segar was further ashamed. Few days later, when Nesan met Segar, the unexpected happened. According to Nesan, had the second baby retained, his wife would not have disobeyed him or challenged him and they would have lived happily. That was an irony Segar had to face.

Once there was a young man creating chaos in the out patient area of the northern town hospital in Sri Lanka. Seeing the crowd Segar stepped in. The young man had his forte viewed by the audience. He was a psychiatric patient known to Segar. When he saw Segar quickly he lowered his tone and tamed. Segar put his arm around the man and took him to psychiatry ward. He was given Pentothal injection and Electro Convulsive Therapy (ECT) against his wish. Whether this was treatment or punishment was the debate of some doctors and nurses. The public viewed this as punishment. Some of Segar's past actions of tying a drunken person to a pillar were recollected. Did Segar who was a human rights activist violate the human rights of that man? Segar thought it would be in his interest to be tamed so that he did not get in to further trouble where he could be physically assaulted by people without knowing he was a psychiatric patient. Segar's experience in administering ECT, zero tolerance for alcohol or commotion, knowing the patient and impulsive decision led to the drastic measure and different interpretations by others. In the northern town hospital, there was a nurse who had no child even after few years of marriage. Other nurses sympathized with her and helped to avoid maternity ward where the nurse could feel more depressed. Once there was an unmarried girl delivered a bay at home assisted by the midwife from Segar's team. Due to social stigma, such babies are disposed by the mother or through others. The midwife was asked by the mother to dispose the baby. The midwife handed over the baby to the childless nurse. The baby was registered as born to the nurse under the very nose of Segar to avoid the hassles of adoption.

MUNICIPAL COUNCIL

After his further studies and blessed with a new born baby, Segar was in dilemma whether to return to his home town to continue his work or not. Segar decided to join the municipal council. The Chief medical officer of health Dr Tissa was an alcoholic and was in the pockets of health inspectors who provided free liquor and food at restaurants which were inspected and licensed by the very same people. Segar who was dedicated and strict disciplinarian could not function independently among these gangsters. Segar never blamed the health inspectors who had to survive with an alcoholic boss. Dr. Tissa removed the re-employed Dr Uragoda who had been an assistant director in ministry of health. Dr Ura was not ready to toe the alcoholic's line since he was a man of principle and integrity. Other elderly doctors were also re-employed after retirement but turned a blind eye to the boss just to survive. Tissa would bypass Segar and request a health inspector to arrange for free alcohol and food since Segar was a teetotaller and a man of integrity. There was a surprise in a meeting just after the transfers of health inspectors. Peiris was a decent health inspector working under Segar. He was ready to leave the job and migrate to Italy. In the meeting, Peiris did not mince his words. He referred to Tissa as alcoholic and a cheap commodity. He said he was not prepared to carry torch for Tissa and was punished during health inspectors' transfer.

SEYCHELLES

Segar found it was embarrassing and humiliation to work in Colombo municipal council under the alcoholic Tissa. Segar found a job in Seychelles and vanished with his wife and the toddler son. Again this was from the frying pan to the fire for Segar. The foreign doctors in primary health care had to work under local nursing officer. The head strong, outspoken and aggressive Segar's confrontation started within 6 months with the nursing officer. She was interfering who should get sick leave and antibiotic. Every Monday morning about 50% of patients were just coming for sick leave with malingering. Segar who was straight forward had to confront few regular malingerers. The island mentality of secluded life was prominent in the Afro-French populations. The main island of 10Km by 10 Km had few hills separating the east and west making transport difficult. The island with only 70,000 population (1993) was an expensive tourist destination. They had few mini islands and pristine beaches. The Coco-De Mer plant and seed was the trade mark of Seychelles. That seed would be an expensive souvenir to any foreigner. Ironically, despite the small population and limited economy they had a national airline. Their source of income was only tourism and fishing. By nature the population was lazy. The white doctors come there for working holiday and do not stay for more than 2 years. The Asian doctors either marry locally and settle or after 5 years claim citizenship so that children get scholarship for overseas studies as they had education only up to year 10. Generally the population was promiscuous and one third of the children were illegitimate according the bishop at that time. The Asians were advised to marry before going there or else marry locally whether voluntarily or due to seduction. The partnerships last for short while among the local population and changing partners was a casual event.

Despite being a small island, their primary health care was totally integrated and a model for other countries which miserably failed in implementing WHO's primary health care. The medical centres functioned as primary health care centres even in the night by syndicating 2 or 3 centres. Even the ambulance service operated from these centres and the doctors were on call at some of these centres. The centre was managed mostly by a nurse during night unless doctor's presence was required. Even at the capital, there was a medical centre close to the general hospital where patients could not go directly. In addition to ambulance service accident and emergency services were also provided by these medical centres. School health and environmental health were also based in these centres. The night calls were mainly the 4As—accident, assault, alcoholism and asthma. They had cheap beer which made several people addicted and resorting to violence and assaults. Politically, the Island was dictatorial after the 1977 coup in which Mancham was overthrown by Rene with the assistance of 500 troops from Tanzanian president Nyerere. Unfortunately after the Soviet collapse they were forced to re-enter democratic stream. Once there was a head line on front page of dailies "You can't eat democracy". Unsurprisingly that was uttered by General Rawlings, the dictator of Ghana when he visited Seychelles.

AGAIN IN CAPITAL

Segar returned to capital from Seychelles after 2 years when he was kicked out by the ministry of health for insubordination to the local nursing officer. Fortunately, Segar could treat his mother's womb cancer in the Sri Lankan capital at no cost with the help of a specialist. Segar used the holiday break effectively to treat his mother and to plan his future. Segar was awaiting his migration to New Zealand. In the meantime, he joined the private Sulaiman's nursing home in Grand Pass, Colombo. Segar already knew that he would not fit in to commercial health service at the expense of ethics and conscience. He was there for few months until his migration to New Zealand. Again Segar soon found out the immoral and unethical practices. Anyone, with right sided abdominal pain would be advised admission and surgery for appendix. Thereafter only, the differential diagnosis of urine infection or kidney ailment would be investigated. Surgery brought more money to the hospital, surgeon, anaesthetist and the doctors. Therefore, the doctors at the front line were interested more in surgery. Whenever a front line doctor referred a patient for surgery, the doctor received a kickback from the surgeon. No doctor was immune from this unethical practice though the hospital was not responsible for this. That was a secret dealing between the referring doctor and the surgeon. There were surgeons ShameJeya, ShameSiri and even the popular surgeon and later vice chancellor Dr PR Anton. The surgeons usually got rupees 3,000 as there (1995) fee out of which rupees 500 was the kickback from the surgeon to the referring doctor without the knowledge of the hospital. The front line doctor got another rupees 500 when he assisted the surgeon during surgery. This could be a doctor other than the doctor who referred the patient.

NEW ZEALAND

Few months later Segar migrated to New Zealand. The new country gave freedom of speech and a relaxed life for Segar while he was pursuing further studies at the Wellington medical school. Once, Segar wrote to immigration department that their application form for visit visa had few errors. There was a kind acknowledgement for pinpointing the errors but would be rectified only during next printing. Going back to university gave a new opportunity to Segar to engage with locals in argument and logic. Segar identified himself with the minority Maori who were the natives of New Zealand. There were open debates about minority and reconciliation or integration of minority with the main stream. Any new migrant also could participate in the forum. Even permanent residents without citizenship were eligible to vote at elections unlike Australia. There was only one difference between permanent residents and citizens. The citizenship was required only to join defence forces.

The native Maori called the settlers as 'Pakeha'. There was an agreement between the Maori queen and the British settlers. However, the settlers used various methods to decimate the natives. The popular divide and rule policy of the British was practised very efficiently. The Maori would be given a gun by the settlers if he brought a head of his own brethren. The thrill and power of gun blinded the Maori who killed their own people to please the settlers. The settlers directly killed thousands of native Maori. The settlers introduced Measles and other infectious diseases to the local population which did not have previous exposure or immunity. Smoking, alcohol and other drugs were introduced in the country that the Maori were disproportionately affected. Thus the number of natives gradually got reduced making life easier for the settlers. The Maori learnt English and their mother tongue usage was also getting reduced. The Maori always identified themselves with a mountain and a river. Unfortunately, they migrated towards cities and towns and lost their identity. Losing the territory and language made the Maori a vulnerable minority depending on the settlers. Pacific islanders especially Samoans too migrated to New Zealand and made the Maori more vulnerable. The settlers thought the Maori were not civilized and rude people but Maori thought the islanders were rough people. The multiculturalism could be seen in Rugby and soccer with islanders shining.

New Zealand, having only 4 million population as compared to the Australian 22 million, followed Australia in many aspects. Except that the first settlers in Australia were out casted convicts, the settlers in both countries followed the same systematic annihilation of the local population, their language, culture and treasures. Therefore, New Zealand and Australia following same path was not astonishing. Compared to Australia, New Zealand had more than 80 million sheep. Their income sources were dairy, wool and tourism. The British call the Kiwis as men from the bush. That was because in many official functions, the Maori welcome of Haka was included for name sake to give the impression of multiculturalism and reconciliation between settlers and natives. The Maori Haka is a type of ancient war dance traditionally used on the battlefield, as well as when welcoming new comers. It would be very intimidating and humiliating but at the end there would be nose kissing and friendliness. The Maori were civilized and had a queen for their collectiveness unlike the Aboriginals of Australia. Further, the Maori resembled the Pacific islanders to some extent and none so ever with Africans whereas the Aboriginals of Australia were mainly descendants of Africans but with straight hair and no hanging lips. From time to time Maori rioted against the settlers rule but every time it was put down with brutal force. The spear, bow and arrow were no match for the invaders' guns and cannons.

The Maori had few in higher positions of the main stream but they were all symbolic and the Maori still lived as second class citizens. Unlike Australia, the debate of colonialism and the fate of Maori were not taboo but encouraged at many forums. Ironically, the racism and white supremacy had been again and again demonstrated in New Zealand society by conscientious white researchers whether it was in housing, tenancy or in employment. The racist Pauline Hanson was decimated after a short glitter in Australia. But in New Zealand the half Maori Winston Peter's party which capitalized on immigration, became the prime mover. This led Winston to become the deputy prime minister. Unfortunately, the power of the party was used to maximize the strength of Winston and his party but not that of native Maori. The constitution, national flag and national anthem were propagating and perpetuating colonialism and white supremacy as they were alien to sons of soil. Many Kiwis migrate to Australia permanently or temporarily. There was a rumour that Lady Hadley was having a lesbian relationship with Anita McNaught. Immediately, Anita left New Zealand and joined BBC. When Al Jazeera started she moved in as a reporter. Her partner of Fox news was kidnapped in Gaza. After 2 weeks he was released as an Islamic Covert under duress. Many from BBC and CNN joined Al Jazeera perhaps due to higher pay. While Segar was pursuing further studies in Wellington, he was offered a job in Brunei Darussalam.

BRUNEI DARUSSALAM

Segar moved to Brunei while leaving his family behind in New Zealand to obtain the citizenship which was conferred after 3 years of residency while Australia offered at the end of only 2 years. Brunei was a small country under British protection. They never accepted that Brunei was a British colony but a British protectorate. However, they gained full independence in January 1984 taking over external affairs and defence as well. Despite the independence a British battalion of Ghurkha regiment was stationed in Brunei under the Brunei—British defence pact. This was because of the rebellion in1962 against the monarchy with assistance from Indonesia's General

Suharno. Being a small country with 300 thousand population in Borneo island surrounded by east Malaysia's Sabah and Sarawak and Indonesia's Kalimantan, the Brunei faced serious threats for its sovereignty. The history of 1962 rebellion and Indonesia's involvement reminded the monarchy all the time the threat faced by them.

The people of Brunei were Malays as in the Malayan peninsula and most of Indonesia. They were mostly Muslims with a minority of Chinese and few Indians. The Ibans, Dusun and Murut tribes were the natives of Brunei and the Malays migrated to Brunei from an Indonesian island. According to Dandan, 10% of the population were known as Pengirans or as Hamsa explained had 'royal blood'. They were the descendants of the illegitimate children of royals over the generations but still respected over the other people. Even the Royals still had to marry a royal blood though the Sultan had an exemption. Another theory is Himalaya (Malaya-Malay) tribes feared the Mongol Genghis Khan and migrated towards Malaya as the Malay people have some resemblance to Ghurkhas Indo Chinese appearance. Historically, Brunei had been a Hindu country until the Mogul empire expanded in the 15th century. When the monarch was converted to Islam, the subjects were also converted to Islam. Though the religion practised is Islam, most of the rituals and ceremonies of the palace still remind the Indian Hindu traditions. Muslims worship with both fists open and held in front of chest. But in palace during ceremonies the Hindu style of both palms made in to a tower in front of chest or on the head was practised. The Malays did not have a script until the arrival of Islam. The Arabic script was used in Malay language and was called Jawi. The British introduced the English alphabet to Malay language which was widely used. But still, in religious classes Jawi is taught. The only English daily Borneo Bulletin was edited by a Sri Lankan, Rex de Silva. Some years back, he had an affair with the wife of Burmese Ambassador in Sri Lanka. One day, in 1972 the Ambassador Boonwat shot dead his wife and diplomatic immunity protected him though he was recalled. He claimed that the firing was accidental. The logic he sought to prove himself was very interesting. He said that had he wanted to kill his wife, he would have done that few times when he saw his wife in bed with Rex de Silva.

The Malays of Brunei are passionate of their language Malay and the religion Islam. Fortunately, the monarchy combined the 3 sacred issues as MIB as referring to Malay language, Islam religion and the political system monarchy. The sacrosanct MIB prohibits any thought or words or action against monarchy. Islam gave only one way passport and it would be a lethal mistake to convert again from Islam. Naturally, the people would be fond of their language. Whether monarchy was revered or not whether liked or not, when the MIB was accepted, the people automatically accepted monarchy even in this modern era. Dandan opined that the Bruneians were stupid because they accepted monarchy. He was a free thinker as compared to atheist and against Islam as well. Surely, he would have contested elections in a democracy. However, unless he was ready to leave the country for ever or ready to be in prison for life, no one would dare to go against monarchy. In effect, Islam and Malay language had been used to control the population by monarch. Islam did not permit liberalism or variations and with 100 per cent loyalty, was effective tool to control political discourse. Those who advocate that Islam was for monarchy or autocracy and against democracy should look at the history and geography. It was true several Arab countries followed monarchy and Pakistan was an example where democracy could not be sustained. However, the Buddhist countries like Thailand and South Korea had their spells of autocracy or military rule. Myanmar, the Buddhist country with 60 years long military rule never had a taste of democracy.

As long as people get at least 2 meals a day and MIB is revered, the monarchy has no apparent threat. Ironically, there is a parliament house in the capital which is hardly used. Occasionally, monarchy appointed representatives assemble there to discuss how to perpetuate MIB and monarchy. The appointments to public service have some shocks from time to time as some wins the lottery without any merit but at the whims and fancies of the monarch. The heads of public service are kept in perpetual instability to ensure the omnipotence of the monarch. The frequent rotation of ministers ensures that no person or personality can have upper hand or be close to the monarch for life. The village heads and heads for cluster of villages were all appointed with the monarch's gospel or 'Titah". Lately, the monarchy introduced election to the village heads. There is no politics in Brunei as the secret service or internal security division ensures total obedience is practised. The criminal prison is manned and visited even by expatriate doctors but the political prison is visited only by local doctors who could not dare to leave the country or seek asylum.

The monarchy of Brunei had been different from the British monarchy. The Sultan hand shakes with bare hand and visits a village every month and takes group photograph with the rural masses. The British queen had been out of touch with the masses and would shake hands with gloves even in hot summer. The Sultan shakes hand with thousands of people on his birthday and during the open house of the palace for Ramadan. Despite the age, with slim and fit body and a pleasant smile all the time he could walk faster than many youth. His PR is very good with visits to every corner and being in touch with masses as compared to the secluded British monarch. Even in this conservative Islamic society where Shari law was practised, the women could drive and work. Many women were clerks in government service with little wages. The women cover their head, cheeks and lower jaw like Egyptians but not like the Saudis. Even men wear long sleeves in formal functions. Segar never saw a Malay in shorts except the tourism chief Sheik Kamal. But the Chinese and Indians as well as foreigners had the freedom of erring short skirts and tight T shirts.

The Sharia law was enforced only for Muslims and not for foreigners or non Muslim locals. There are several churches still and two Hindu temples of the Ghurkha regiments. Locals as well as foreigners have the freedom to practise their own faith except that conversion was not permitted. Only the government could convert one way from other religions to Islam. Some foreigners especially Filipinos and some British convert to marry a Muslim woman. In Indonesia, a non Muslim could marry a Muslim without converting to Islam. But in Brunei, under Sharia law a Muslim could not be married to a non Muslim. The couple would be given 2 choices, the non Muslim to convert to Islam or the couple should leave Brunei. According to Sharia law, a woman could not be the head of a family as such that even foreign women do not get the family visa or children's education allowance paid by the government unless she was a widower or a divorcee. Other than this the foreigners have absolute freedom to practise their own faith unlike in Saudi Arabia. Segar being a government officer had to follow the government regulations and should start any meeting with Islamic prayer. However, his freedom to remain a Hindu was never challenged or threatened. During floods, once, Segar attended a meeting convened by the district administrator in a mosque as a free Hindu.

The Malays are gentle and pleasant people unlike the Seychelles' island mentality. Malays are friendly but women usually do not shake hands with men except their immediate family. Dandan was implying that Segar, travelling in a car with a non Muslim woman too contributed to 'kalwat" or adultery according to Sharia. The kalwat offence does not apply to 2 non muslims and several Filipinos and British take advantage of that. However when a non Muslim was alone with a Muslim woman, it could mean kalwat if they were found to be in compromising positions. Even then at least 4 witnesses were required to result in an offence. Once, Sergar's 2 staff, a Chinese clerk and a Muslim midwife were alleged to be in relationship in the same clinic. Segar wrote a confidential letter to his bosses about 'kalwat' or adultery. As it was punishable under Sharia law Segar was about to transfer one of them to another clinic. Segar was immediately summoned and told to tear all letters, erase the computer records and just transfer one of the 2 staff without giving any reason what so ever. That was because, the allegation 'kalwat' needed solid evidence and witnesses which could be difficult if none of the staff were ready to provide evidence or witness.

Unfortunately, Segar had an unpleasant experience shortly after he was allocated a house. He was threatened by a built up gentleman with a club that Segar should leave the house. If it was his home country, Segar would have challenged the man and even retaliated. But just 2 months after arrival in a foreign country, Segar took the man to the neighbours. Later Segar found out that he was a teacher and terminated from service due to his mental illness. There was a cold war going on between the land lady and this man and Segar got caught in the proxy war. Other than this incident, Segar felt very safe and comfortable in Brunei for 12 years out of which 8 years as health services district administrator. Respect, kindness and gentleness are the norm for most Malays though some Chinese could be arrogant at times. Segar enjoyed the hospitality and the prestige for 8 years whenever he received a royal or a cabinet minster or a permanent secretary. At one stage Segar became an eye sore and popular than locals. That was the time Segar had grown out of proportion and a local replaced him. The Chinese controlled private sector education and most of commerce. There was an unwritten policy of 'Bhumi Putra' or sons of the soil. Most government positions were given to Malay Muslims but private sector was dominated by Chinese who migrated 100 years ago. Even the business licences were approved for the local Malays but foreigners virtually buy the licence from the local for a monthly commission. Segar had observed this phenomenon even in Saudi Arabia in 1980s. There are some stateless Chinese that they do not have citizenship but permanent residence. A local man could confer citizenship by marriage to the spouse but a woman had no such concession.

During the time Segar remained in Brunei, there were few natural disasters like haze, floods, cholera and hand, foot and mouth disease. However, due to the small population, it was easy to control or take care of the population to contain any disaster. Like Sri Lanka, Brunei has very high coverage of immunisation. In Sri Lanka a single case of Whooping Cough was big news in Segar's territory. In Brunei, an infant of 4 months old had Whooping Cough. Segar and others flew by chopper to investigate the case as it was a serious matter. Compare this with Australia where Segar's son had mild form of Whooping Cough as a teen ager. Fortunately, he had some immunity due to childhood vaccines in other countries. Vaccine preventable diseases are occurring sporadically in the developed Australia as parents do not take immunisation seriously. The Australian Medical Association proposed that without complete immunisation, children should be banned from schools! In Alberta, Canada, Polio outbreaks are common due to religious taboo of some residents.

In 2009, a child died 8 hours after being seen by Segar due to ruptured Appendix. Segar was shaken by the event. Ironically, Segar requested the director to investigate the incident as a precious life was lost. After seeing his notes, Segar gave his response. Unfortunately, none of the staff could remember the particular patient. The child was treated just like any other child. Though triage was blamed, Segar insisted that the diagnosis was missed in the rush as Segar had seen many patients in that session. After the investigation, Segar was exonerated and requested to give a lecture on Childhood Emergencies. However, hurt by the death Segar decided to leave Brunei by the end of the year. At the end of the lecture, Segar quoted several examples of high profile cases where collective responsibility of the hospital doctors miserably missed fatal cases. The school boy was sent home from 3 hospitals leading to the death of the child due to Meningitis or brain fever. The cousin of Segar's wife lost his 40 year old wife in Nepean Hospital Sydney as a private patient due to ovarian cancer in 2005. After removing the tumour, the specialists' board decided no further treatment was required as 13 satellite specimens around the tumour were clear. Preventive chemo was considered unnecessary. Within one year, she died of metastases. A young lady doctor died in Brunei when she was treated with steroids for an auto immune disease. She died of miliary or disseminated tuberculosis. A Pakistani doctor in Brunei had cancer of tongue. He had surgery and radiotherapy. The follow up was done by the ENT surgeon and Oncologist in Brunei. At the end of 2 years, he had vocal cord paralysis and hoarse voice. No CT scan or MRI was done. He was treated with steroid for 'viral infection'. He died of metastases within 9 months. The Israeli prime minister 'Bull' Aerial Sharon had minor stroke. He was poisoned by his doctors with over dose of anti coagulant. He died of brain bleeding. This happened exactly one year after the Israelis poisoned Yasser Arafat.

Electronic health was to be introduced in 2003 but unfortunately, despite the budget allocation of 100 million dollars, it never took off even when Segar left in 2009. The country is 120 km long and 100 km wide with 85% of the population residing along the costal areas. The interior still had mostly Iban, Dusun and Murut tribes who were non Muslims and some women were bare breasted as seen in some parts of Africa. They lived in so called long houses which would have common roof and veranda with private rooms. The cost of living was high compared to neighbouring east Malaysia as such many Bruneians would cross the border to Sarawak or Sabah during weekends for 3 commodities: grocery, alcohol and sex. As an Islamic country, alcohol is banned but non Muslims including foreigners can carry or keep 2 litres and drink whenever they want but not in public places. As a conservative Islamic society, sex without marriage was prohibited to Muslims and this led people to cross to the liberal east Malaysia. The tourist attractions are few like the Kampong Ayer or water village, golden mosque and petroleum industry.

The royals numbering hundred enjoy extravaganza and luxury from the petroleum export but the masses have ordinary life. The number of foreigners working in palace especially Filipinos was more than thousand. General Suharto was over thrown in Indonesia after 36 years when masses could not have 2 square meals. Until then the dictator was tolerated by 250 million people. The Brunei monarchy is aware that as long as ordinary people could have ordinary life without poverty, the monarchy would not be challenged. The monarchy ensures that majority of the subjects had a decent life. There was a play boy prince who was a sex maniac and spendthrift. He could go to any Brunei supermarket and pick up a sales girl from Philippines for his fun. The sales girl would be rewarded generously so that there would be no murmurs or grumbling. He was a megalomaniac who started massive projects for the small nation. The Jerudong theme park, Jerudong private hospital and Jerudong international school were the 3 monsters he created. In, 1997, when this prince was in exile in UK, all 3 projects were collapsing. The free for all theme park was running at barest minimum. The hospital could not be sustained and became medical centre. The school was a massive loss but the government propped up by providing education allowance to parents whose children studied in this school. His company Amedeo mismanaged foreign investment and Brunei wealth. When this company collapsed in 1998, Brunei lost 28 billion dollars. When the prince scooted off to exile, the Islamic clergy and the chief Mufti declared allegiance to the monarch to prevent any rumours or resentment against monarch.

The playboy prince was an outcast for some time. The government filed cases against him in UK and recovered some money. All these were public drama to fool the innocent masses. After few years in exile, the prince joined back the royal family and his photo started to reappear in government brochures. During the case, it was revealed that one of the royal family members required 50 thousand dollars a week for the up keeping. That was the magnitude of the extravaganza of the royals who would have many children each from various marriages. Several austerity measures were introduced to the masses to cut down expenses of the government but the royals' sacrifice was symbolic. The number of luxury vehicles would be a token for the extravaganza of the royal family. All the children of the Royals enjoyed the same luxury. There was Polo just for the royals and a massive hotel 'Empire' exclusively for them. Later on just to sustain, it was opened for the locals and expatriates.

WHAT IS SPECIAL ABOUT AUSTRALIA?

The world has diversified opinions and standards. There may be criticisms about opinion, words or actions. The person who was called terrorist, Nelson Mandela became a modern day Gandhi. The time and place spectrum can modify the value at different points. No human is perfect. The theme of this narrative is what Voltaire expressed candidly: "I do not agree with what you have to say, but I will defend to the death your right to say it." The civilized and matured world appreciates difference of opinions and actions. Sometimes people agree to disagree but respect others' views. In a democratic and pluralist society multiple ideas are promoted · though finally all agree to the majority values. National security and patriotism should not suppress freedom of expression. A maverick or group with a radical view is termed as terrorist or hate campaigner or unpatriotic or even worse, claimed to have incited violence and disharmony. These are tactics to stifle freedom of expression by dictators and monarchs who want to be leader for life without any dissent or challenge. Soviet Union, Russia, China, Zimbabwe, Egypt under Mubarak and Libya under Gadhafi are examples of this category. Even Hitler used Nationalism and patriotism for his ambition. Australia respects freedom of expression and free debate. Australian Liberal Party leader said "Any prohibitions on inciting hatred against or intimidation of particular racial groups should be akin to the ancient common law offences of incitement and causing fear". He was very explicit in emphasising that expression or advocacy should not be prohibited with anti discrimination law (ABC, 7Aug, 2012). In the modern democratic society, freedom of expression is highly valued. The most important value in Australia which Segar appreciated is freedom of expression. This is not a divisive narrative or hate campaign. There is no intention of promoting social disharmony. The anti Islamic propaganda is justified but Aboriginal advocacy is suppressed in Australia in the name of nationalism and patriotism. Please remember what **Voltaire said "I do not agree with what you have to say, but I will defend to the death your right to say it."**